MAGPIE MEMORIES

Conversations with Newcastle players down the decades

by Malcolm Holt

breedon **books**
PUBLISHING

First published in Great Britain in 2004 by

The Breedon Books Publishing Company Limited

Breedon House, 3 The Parker Centre,

Derby, DE21 4SZ.

ISBN 1 85983 421 3

Printed and bound by Scotprint, Haddington, Scotland.

Contents

Acknowledgements

Photographs supplied by Newcastle Chronicle and Journal Limited. To order a copy of a photograph telephone the Photosales Department on 0191 2016001.

THE WARM-UP

NEWCASTLE United Football Club emerged in 1892, although its origins can be traced back to 1881 when a club called Stanley was formed. In 1882, Stanley changed its name to Newcastle East End. Formed in 1882, Newcastle West End played on the site of the current St James' Park. When Newcastle West End ceased to exist in 1889, Newcastle East End were invited to move to their ground. They agreed to the move, later changed their name to Newcastle United, and the rest, as they say, is history.

You could say that I have lived in the 'shadow' of St James' Park, the home of Newcastle United, since the long hot summer of 1976. Perhaps the shadow effect does require a significant slice of journalistic licence, but I can at least walk out of my house and admire the mighty Sir John Hall Stand, a mere mile or so away. The revamped stadium stands proud, overlooking the equally revamped city of Newcastle upon Tyne, and is just as famous worldwide as the Tyne Bridge.

As a teenager growing up in my native East Yorkshire, I cut my football supporter's teeth standing on the terraces of Bunkers Hill at Boothferry Park, watching Hull City playing in the old Third Division. Like all young supporters, I had my heroes. In the mid-1960s, the Tigers were attracting crowds of over 30,000, who marvelled at the silky skills of goalscorers Ken 'Waggy' Wagstaff and Chris Chilton, and Ian Butler flying down the left wing.

I actually made a guest appearance on BBC's *Match of the Day* on one occasion, standing behind the goal when a penalty was awarded. I proudly demonstrated the correct method of using the traditional wooden rattle when the ball hit the back of the net and it was all captured on national television. Of course, wooden rattles are no longer permitted at football matches for fear of supporters knocking some sense into the brains of the opposition, or more likely the loudmouthed 'know all' sitting nearby.

Even during the rollercoaster years of my adolescence, I had already found a second team whose fortunes I followed closely. Therefore, it was perhaps inevitable that when I decided to leave Hull City for a higher division, my destination would be Newcastle United. It was rather unfortunate that as I headed for Tyneside on a free transfer, Malcolm 'Supermac' Macdonald departed to Highbury, following a very public falling out with manager Gordon Lee, for a lot more: £333,333 to be precise. We must have passed each other somewhere on the A1. Sadly, I wasn't driving a Rolls-Royce at the time.

Having lived in Newcastle upon Tyne since the onset of global warming, I consider myself an adopted Geordie. All of my children were born in the city and bleed black and white. Even my pedigree mongrel dog, a former resident of the local Dog and Cat Shelter, has one set of black whiskers and one set of white ones.

The fluctuating fortunes and misfortunes of Newcastle United have been well documented in a variety of recent publications. The annual quest for silverware has continued to fill the collective hearts of the Toon Army faithful with great optimism as each season kicks off. Sadly, expectations have usually not been fulfilled and rival supporters have relished the opportunity to gloat and remind Newcastle United supporters that the last major trophy came in 1969.

Football has always generated its fair share of heroes, more often than not the players who score spectacular goals that win matches. When I played schoolboy football, I was an old-fashioned centre-half and as such, I admired the robust talents of professional defenders. On many occasions 'the man of the match' award is given to the goalscorers rather than the real playmakers, who perhaps really deserve it.

I commenced my amateur journalistic journey with Newcastle United by penning an article for *The Mag*, the most successful Toon Army supporters' fanzine, following the second coming of Kevin Keegan, who filled the manager's seat in 1992. There followed many published articles over several seasons. This book was born out of an attempt to try something different.

I had been busy tracking down many former Newcastle United players for a family autograph collection and this detective work had proved to be as exciting as it was challenging. My first interview arose from initial contact with a player for an autograph. It proved to be a fascinating encounter, with stories of highs and lows, and entertaining anecdotes from the same era during which I was attending Boothferry Park as a youngster.

I had decided to interview a former player from the 1960s for a new magazine article and we met one Saturday morning for a chat. It soon became apparent that, having acquired almost an hour of material, condensing it onto one page was going to be impossible. A book was born.

Magpie Memories reflects the reality of the research. I spent many happy and fascinating hours, sometimes sitting in the homes of former players, drinking coffee and talking football. Their collective accounts cover the years

1944–1998, during which time all aspects of the 'beautiful game' changed dramatically.

The players featured in this book encountered mixed fortunes during their playing careers, but all of them earned the right to wear the Newcastle United shirt. They were all dedicated to the 'Black and White' cause during their days at St James' Park. Some of them made no effort to disguise their emotions when recalling their memories of specific moments in their careers.

Charlie Crowe played left-half during the period 1944–57. Not one to seek the headlines, Charlie was a true grafter, always giving maximum effort and believing in playing the game the way it should be played. Charlie qualified as an FA coach and was an FA Cup winner with Newcastle United in 1951. He sadly missed out on playing in the 1955 FA Cup Final victory due to injury.

George Luke played outside-left during two periods, 1950–53 and 1959–61. A promising schoolboy international, George later played in the shadow of more experienced players at Newcastle United during his first spell and on his return, by his own admission, he never reached his full potential.

Bobby Cummings, like George Luke, had two spells at Newcastle, playing as a centre-forward during the periods 1954–56 and 1963–65. After a disappointing time as a junior, Bobby returned and contributed significantly to Newcastle's Second Division Championship run in the 1964–65 season.

Bobby Moncur played centre-half during the period 1960–74. After an unsettled start, Bobby went on to captain Newcastle United with distinction and is still best remembered for leading the team to victory in the Inter Cities Fairs Cup in 1969.

Dave Hilley played inside-forward during the period 1962–67. Following promotion back to the First Division, Dave played in every league match for Newcastle United during the 1965–66 season. Dave still visits St James' Park regularly, writing match reports for a Sunday newspaper.

Ron McGarry played centre-forward and inside-forward during the period 1962–67. A powerful player, Ron was one of the real characters in the game at that time. He was always the joker in the pack and gave out calling cards to opposing defenders.

Gordon Marshall was goalkeeper during the period 1963–68. Tall and brave, Gordon was between the posts for all Newcastle United's league games during the Second Division Championship winning season 1964–65.

Wyn Davies played centre-forward during the period 1966–71. He was given the nicknames 'Wyn the Leap' and 'The Welsh Flyer' when playing for Newcastle United. Wyn played a vital role in the Inter Cities Fairs Cup victory in 1969 and was Newcastle United's top goalscorer in European competitions, scoring 10 goals.

Keith Dyson was a striker during the period 1967–71. Keith developed a workmanlike partnership with Wyn Davies, playing in the First Division and the three consecutive Inter Cities Fairs Cup campaigns from 1968 to 1971.

Nigel Walker was a midfield player during the period 1977–82. A gifted player, Nigel suffered from playing in less successful sides and was not given the opportunity to realise his full potential.

David McCreery was a midfield player during the period 1982–89. David was a no-nonsense midfield general, who once declared that it was his job to win the ball and give it to someone else. Getting hurt doing his job was just part of the game as far as David was concerned.

John Beresford played left-back during the period 1992–98. 'Bez' was signed by Kevin Keegan and became one of the 'Entertainers', as Newcastle United became known during Keegan's reign. He also played under Kenny Dalglish and scored some crucial goals in the Champions League.

None of the players in this book went on to become multi-millionaires like some of the modern day superstars. However, they all knew that they could contribute something unique to the history of Newcastle United and were delighted to have been given the opportunity to demonstrate their footballing skills.

Football has become a big business, with huge transfer deals and some players receiving thousands of pounds each week. Sadly, the game has been tarnished in more recent times by events off the field, many of which were influenced by the trappings of fame and fortune. The players in this book experienced varying levels of fame, but nothing as great or intrusive as many in the spotlight today.

The interviews carried out for this book between August 2003 and January 2004 have enabled me to complete an amazing journey through time, from the FA Cup victories in the 1950s, the Fairs Cup victory in 1969, the ups and downs of the 1970s and 1980s, to the rollercoaster Keegan era of the

'Entertainers' in the 1990s. Throughout this journey, I have welcomed the support of my family, who have embraced my passion for football over many years. I am also grateful to my colleague and fellow Newcastle United supporter Allan Jacques for his constructive comments and personal support throughout the preparation of this book. My literary journey also provided a timely reminder that football should after all be a skilful game played with a ball by 22 players.

In this book, I have tried to cover all areas of the football pitch by interviewing former players from goalkeeper to centre-forward. I hope that the players' recollections of their times on the pitch will help readers to recall their own off the pitch. I am immensely grateful to all the players who happily gave up their valuable time to talk to me and to share their experiences. These are their Magpie memories in 'black and white'.

Chapter 1

CHARLIE CROWE
(1944–57)

CHARLES Alfred Crowe was born in Walker, Newcastle upon Tyne, on 30 October 1924. Charlie signed for Newcastle United in October 1944 for the grand sum of £10. He played left-half for 13 years, making 216 first-team appearances and scoring seven goals. He was an FA Cup winner with Newcastle United in 1951, but sadly missed out on playing in the 1955 final through an ankle injury, even though Jackie Milburn famously offered him the chance to be carried through the game by his teammates.

Charlie's football career began when he was still at school and his first job surprised one of his relatives.

'It just happened. I played for my schoolboy team, Victoria Jubilee in Byker, and I was proud of it. I was born in a battlefield. I had three uncles who worked at the docks on the quayside. The very first job that I had at 15½ was at the Tyne Tees Shipping Company and I got a job in the office. My uncles didn't know that I'd taken over the job, which was paying the stevedores and the other workers. My Uncle Dick came to the window one day and you would have thought someone had hit him with a bomb. He said "Charlie, what are you doing here?" "Oh", I said, "I'm doing the wages". He took a small coin out of his packet, sixpence or a shilling, and he said "That's for you, but don't tell your Aunt Bessie". I had numerous jobs, myself, but the one that I wanted to stop in was playing football.'

Charlie made his professional debut playing for Newcastle United against Stoke City when the football leagues had been suspended because of World War Two. Although the game was a special occasion for Charlie, it was remembered by him just as much for the goal-scoring exploits of an exceptional player who was to become a close friend in later years.

'When I made my debut, it was against Stoke City and we won 9–1, with Albert Stubbins scoring five goals. He scored three times in the first 15 minutes. I had a special man-marking job to do. It was to mark Stanley Matthews. So, I had a free-kick to take. I put the ball down warily, thinking to myself, where is he? Anyway, I eventually took the kick, there had been a bit of general play, the ball came over and I didn't play for any particular player. But, at the far post, there was Albert, he was up like a swan and he ricocheted this ball, bang into the net.

'Mind, I had a real setback not so long ago, when Albert Stubbins died. I missed him loads. We used to go into town, into Northumberland Street, Marks and Sparks, in the restaurant, and we used to put the football world to rights. Albert was a good talker and a nice lad. He just popped away one day. He was still the same size and Arsenal was still his favourite team. A lot of people didn't know that Albert was once the manager of a soccer crowd in America. He was the first manager there. He loved New York, he loved it.'

The team was the New York Americans and Albert Stubbins managed them in 1960. Albert had played for Newcastle United, Liverpool, and England, and was also famous for appearing on the cover of the Beatles' album *Sergeant Pepper's Lonely Hearts Club Band.*

When he retired, Charlie took up residence in the Longbenton area of Newcastle and now lives a short distance from Newcastle United's new purpose-built training facility. I asked Charlie to recall his memories of training at Newcastle United in the late 1940s.

'We did all our training at St James' Park, apart from at the beginning of the season. Then we used to run marathons round the Town Moor, up into Gosforth, and back down to Leazes. And that was that. As a matter of fact, Tommy Swinburne, the goalkeeper, didn't like to run round there. He was a goalkeeper. He used to say "I don't run anywhere near them". We left him alone. The trainers couldn't do anything with him. He used to take his pipe and his paper, he would go onto the Town Moor, find a nice seat, sit down, read his paper, then come back again. That was all that he did.

'But, we also used to go round about 10 to 15 laps of the perimeter of the pitch, and then about 12 to 20 sprints, 80 yarders or 100 yarders. We would see who was the fastest, but that was about all. We wanted to play five-a-side on the field, but it was taboo. We couldn't get a game, we couldn't be on the grass at St James' Park. It was sacred.

'The first week out from that system, it was training on the cement in the car park. Tommy Walker slipped one day and broke his arm, so they had a little rethink about using the car park and it just died a death. The early part of the season, that's all we did, laps around the track, to keep yourself in good shape.'

There have always been stories that professional footballers are a superstitious bunch and seemingly in the 1940s and 1950s they were pretty much the same. Charlie remembered that some players had little rituals when he talked about matchdays. His own particular ritual was quite unique and unusual.

'There was really only one lad who was superstitious, that was Jackie [Milburn]. I used to roll my sleeves up and get the outside-right to take them down. Then the winger had to put them back up. It was Tommy Walker as a matter of fact. Also, Joe Harvey kept a coin. He always used to keep it in his pocket. Apart from that, there was no magic. I would just leave the house, make my way to town after a cup of tea and some breakfast. We nearly always had the same meal at the County.'

Being the manager of Newcastle United has always put people in the public spotlight, just as much as it does for the players. The quality of managers at Newcastle United has varied over recent years and it was no different when Charlie played, as he recalled.

'When it came to the managerial side, we had some terrible managers. They think that because they pass a coaching course… I almost fell out with Bobby Mitchell once. It was down to Dugald Livingstone. He said "Charlie, I've noticed that you're getting stereotyped in your play, your balls to Bobby Mitchell". I said "That's the way that he wants them". He called Bobby over and he said "I've just told Charlie he's going to use the bisecting pass". He looked at me and we ran out onto the park. Bobby said straight away "If you think that I'm going to do anything like this, I'm not going to run for the ball and I'm going to make you look a fool because I'll run out of the way of it". I said "Aye, we'll just play our own game". He said "Aye, we better had".

'I think I could find Bobby Mitchell with a pass in the dark. Not because I was a good player, but because of Mitch's way of creating space, his own space. He could sell a dummy once or twice, or whatever. There were some tremendous characters in the 1951 side. Mind you, the managers' talk-ins were my dreams for writing stuff.

'Stan Seymour would come in and say "All the best for today, boys. You're playing for Newcastle United, so you're all good enough, right?" It was stupid stuff. Dugald Livingstone used to have us jumping over Olympic-style hurdles on the concrete outside the players' entrance and heading imaginary balls. Well, I was a qualified staff coach and I was thinking to myself… well, never mind.

'Bobby Mitchell said "Charlie, we'll have to have a talk. This fella's a cracker". This was before Dugald Livingstone went out with a ball and a piece of chalk and marked something on one of the panels. We were all standing around. We had done our laps and were wondering what was going on with Dugald pontificating. Well, Mitch said "Where are you going tonight?" He took no notice at all. Dugald came round and there was Ivor Broadis, Len White, Jackie Milburn, George Robledo, and he showed them how to kick a ball. In fact, I couldn't believe my eyes. I couldn't believe that anybody in their right mind would do that, particularly to international natural kickers of the ball.

'Of course, he looked at me when one or two of the lads started to laugh. He looked straight at me and he said "You should know all about this, being a coach". I said "Staff coach. I don't even teach five-year-old boys how to kick a ball, because they kick it just naturally and they want to enjoy it". So, Mitch said to me "I'll bet you get dropped on Saturday". I did as well and it taught me a lesson. As a matter of fact, it didn't matter, because I was the first player to have a full-time job. I still did all the training.

'During a tactical talk, George Martin once said to Bobby Mitchell "Do you have anything to contribute to my talk?" He said "Aye, what's a six letter word for so and so?" He was doing a crossword. It was ways and means. You just had to go there when you played football. You just get wrapped up in it.'

Newcastle United supporters have always been known for their fanatical support of their team and when Charlie graced St James' Park, many of the crowds were bigger than those of today. I asked for his thoughts about the supporters of Newcastle United during his playing days.

'When you ran out at St James' Park, the hairs on the back of your neck stood up. Wembley didn't do anything for me. I was pleased to be playing there, but it did nothing for me. The Geordies make more noise than Wembley when you run out at home. They always did.

'Mind you, they used to have their quips, of course. You couldn't play brilliantly all the time. If you misplaced any passes or something, one or two would be getting at you, but it was all with humour. "What's the matter with your lass?" or "Did you have a drink too many last night?" As they're saying these things, they're giving you the ball for a throw-in. Aye, they were smashing, the supporters.'

Charlie scored seven goals for Newcastle United. I asked him if he had a favourite.

'There was one when we went on to the Cup Final in 1951. We played at Bristol Rovers. It was a mudheap. They had to put the greyhound racing off, which shows you what it was like when we walked out onto the pitch. Anyway, the ball had been switched to Joe Harvey and he set Bobby Mitchell away. It was the sixth round and at St James' they had played like devils. They ran and ran and ran. We were extremely fortunate to get even a draw. One of their players hit the post in the last minute. Jack Fairbrother's smile was huge.

'They were a Third Division side and we had taken the game too lightly. We just ran about, but it didn't happen. But, when we went down there for the replay, we were right on the mark. The goal that sealed it and kept us on route to Wembley, the ball had gone to Joe Harvey, back to Mitch, Mitch sent it straight across the park, and it submerged in the penalty area. I was just running up and it went straight in. That was the winner, but it is always a team game.'

Newcastle United won the FA Cup on three occasions in the 1950s and although they have played in subsequent finals, that earlier success has never been matched. Charlie's career with Newcastle spanned those glorious early 1950s, at a time when the closeness of the players was evident. Charlie had so many great memories to recall and choosing a favourite performance proved to be difficult.

'There are that many. There was Wembley in 1951, but there are that many. There was always the banter with the players to each other. There were never any jealousies. The majority of the lads were pit boys. We got on well and that made our performances that bit special.'

I asked Charlie to recall his favourite players and personal heroes.

'Ernie Taylor was the best of the lot for my money. All inside-forwards, quite smallish with great skills, they were usually very clever. You had to be on your toes. Even against Stan Matthews, I didn't win the whole lot. I was very lucky to break even with him.

'I don't think that I had one particular hero. The one player who I liked a lot was little Hughie Gallacher and he was my father's favourite player. When I started playing football, Hughie was playing for Gateshead. He was over the hill, but he was a nice man. Little Ernie Taylor and I got on really well with him. We used to stop on after home games and have a couple of beers with him. He was a magnificent player as well. You've got to be a class player to play for your country at left-half and inside-left.'

Charlie was a tough player on the pitch, but he has always been a gentleman both on and off it. It is not surprising that he was a little embarrassed when recalling one particular incident.

'It was poor Jessie Pye of Wolverhampton Wanderers, he was a class player, an inside-forward. The ball had run out of play when I was with him. It hadn't actually gone in the crowd. Jessie went and got the ball and gave it to me. I was still on the line and when I looked down the field, there he was, a big strong lad with a large back. I threw the ball against his back and it came back to me, obviously. I went away and put the ball through to little Ernie. I think that we scored from it.

'I didn't know what to do. I went in the dressing room at the finish and I said "I'm awfully sorry". He took it all in good spirits. It's part and parcel of the game, but you don't really do these things. It was the first time and the only time that I was ashamed of myself.'

Charlie appeared on the recently released *Newcastle United. The Official History* video and he has also produced two books featuring his days at St James' Park. Charlie continues to make special appearances at St James' Park, as he explained.

'Bobby Moncur rang me up about three weeks ago. He said "Charlie, we haven't had you up here for a while, do you fancy coming up?" He does this thing with the Heroes. I said yes and he said "Well, you will be my guest". So, I went up there and in fact, the following day Ronnie Simpson came down. I was at the Birmingham game and Bobby said "Will you walk with me through the hospitality rooms?" Well, those hospitality rooms are pretty big and I had a microphone. I've never been happy with a microphone, but never mind. He stuck one in my hand and he said "I'll tell you what I'll do. I'll just ask you a few questions".

'His first question was "What was Joe Harvey like as a manager?" I said "Well, I never played underneath him as a player, but I played with him as a player. When he first came to Newcastle, he had the record transfer fee of £4,250, and he was a sergeant major in the Army. He didn't take any prisoners on the park either and he had a bad temper. If you were alright with him, you were alright with the club".

'I was under a bit of a misapprehension when Joe came to Newcastle, because when he arrived he said that he thought that he had joined a boys club team. Actually we were all 16, 17, or 18 and that was what he meant. Anyway, Bobby said "What were you saying? You were under a bit of a misapprehension. I used to be terrified of him and I was his captain". That was Joe.'

Charlie Crowe was a great servant to Newcastle United during his 13 years at the club. It seems somewhat appropriate to finish with one of his early memories of playing schoolboy football and a quote that perhaps summed up his career.

'I was playing for Newcastle Boys against Wallsend Boys and in the paper it said "The diminutive Crowe excelled in all departments". I kept that one and put it in the old scrapbook.'

Chapter 2

GEORGE LUKE
(1950–53, 1959–61)

GEORGE Thomas Luke was born in Newcastle upon Tyne on 17 December 1933. He first signed for Newcastle United as a youngster in December 1950 and stayed with the club until October 1953, when he moved to Hartlepools United. At that time, present-day Hartlepool were called Hartlepools. George signed for Newcastle United for a second time in October

1959 and stayed until January 1961. Playing as an outside-left, George made a total of 29 first-team appearances and scored four goals. He began his football career playing for Newcastle Boys at an early age.

'As a schoolboy, the records will tell you that I showed a lot of potential. I played for Newcastle Boys from about nine and a half right the way through to 15. Getting into the England set-up, I was reserve for England at St James' Park and I went from there and graduated through Newcastle Reserves at 17 when I signed professional. It was during the days of 1951–53 seasons, when it was always drummed into our heads that you had to serve your time. There weren't many footballers that were classed as being really good at 17 years of age. You couldn't get into the first team.

'I was in the Reserves and I was doing quite well, and they came along and said "We want you to go to Hartlepool for a bit of experience. You're going to get a first-team game." So, I went down to Hartlepool at 19 and I thoroughly enjoyed it. I was part-time there for a while because I didn't really turn full-time until I finished my time as a plumber at 21. I stayed down at Hartlepool until I was 22, when the records will show that Newcastle United were chasing me because I scored 22 goals this particular season. The papers were full of it and so and so, and that was from the outside-left position, not as they play today. Newcastle came back after me and I came back.

'Now, that was in the day when Bobby Mitchell was just on his way out. In fact, Bobby played left-half and they put me at outside-left. My first game, that I can remember, was against Fulham away. Then we played against Everton the next week and we beat them 8–2. I scored the first goal.'

Training programmes have changed significantly over the

years. When George played in the 1950s, training seemed to lack the finesse of the modern era.

'When you talk about the training side of it, we were off on a Monday, came in on a Tuesday, and we'd have a game, first team against the Reserves at St James' Park. Charlie Mitten was the manager at that time. Wednesday was taken up with the average running and exercises, and Thursday was when we used to get the ball out and play on the car park in front of St James' Park. We'd hammer each other to bits on there in the rain and everything, and I've seen some lads really injured in those games. Then on Friday, we did general exercises and a few sprints, got paid, and off we went if we were travelling away, or back home and in for the game on the Saturday.'

George recalled the build-up to games at St James' Park as a very anxious experience.

'I had a very, very nervous time. When I came back to Newcastle, it seemed to affect me a bit, that all of a sudden I was jumping from playing in front of 4–6,000 crowds with Hartlepool to 30–50,000 at Newcastle. I always remember on the Saturday morning of the first home match, I couldn't talk to anybody. I didn't want to talk to anyone, even at home. I just wanted to be on my own. The nerves in my tummy were just absolutely tremendous. I used to go to the toilet about 10 or 15 times before a match and have little pees. It was a really nervous kind of thing. It's true, a lot of footballers say that even if you haven't got any nerves, it's normal for you to have these, and I certainly did.

'It was one of those things that as the game built up, we used to go for lunches first and at two o'clock we would get the blackboard out and chat about strategies for the game, what was going to happen and what we were going to do.

Then it would be back to the nerves as you got changed out of your clothes and put the strip on.

'Once you put your foot on that pitch, the nerves just went. Something just happened. Those kinds of thing just disappeared. All of Saturday morning was a tremendous effort for me. It was like sap draining out of your body. It was an experience that I never had at Hartlepool. It was mainly because of the crowd. At St James' Park in those days, you could hear the crowd coming in, you could hear them jumping up and down, because the stand was more or less just above you. It was very nerve-wracking for me.'

At the start of his football career, George showed great potential. However, things didn't work out as well as expected. He recalled his own disappointment.

'I was always very pleased with the way I looked as if I was going to make the grade when I was a schoolboy and a junior. I never ever reached that potential at Newcastle, which was the biggest disappointment of my life. I reached it at Hartlepool in that one season. Well, I had some good seasons at Hartlepool, I must admit. For a left-winger, to score 22 goals in one of those seasons, you were a good player. When I came back to Newcastle, I thought, right, I could go on from there. But, the unfortunate thing was that when I was playing for Hartlepool, I had a very bad accident. It was the same kind of thing that Paul Gascoigne had. My cruciate ligaments went and in those days, you either had good legs, good strong legs, muscular legs, or you were forced to pack the game in. In fact, two notable surgeons told me that maybe I would never kick a ball again.

'I proved them wrong and I came back with Hartlepool and after that, I got transferred back to Newcastle, but that extra yard of pace was missing. I didn't seem to get it back.

The jump from the Third Division North to the First Division, as it was then, was probably just a little too much, and while I held my own for a little while, I was picked if I wasn't injured. I was really disappointed that I never did what I wanted to do. As a schoolboy, you wanted to be a Jackie Milburn. He was a good pal of mine. You wanted to be that kind of a star. Honestly, I was really disappointed that I never showed what I could have done.'

George scored four goals for Newcastle United. He recalled his favourite.

'I didn't score too many goals for Newcastle, to be honest with you. In the first home game back for Newcastle against Everton, when we beat them 8–2, I scored my first goal. I was really on top form and I felt good, and I had quite a good game. I think Gordon Hughes put a centre across from the right and it broke out, coming on to my right foot. Ivor Allchurch and I were going for the ball, and I shouted "Leave it!" and I cracked it. It flew into the top right-hand corner. It makes you feel good. It was early on in the game, so it stirred you up. We went on to win a very good game.'

I asked George to relive some of his more memorable games playing for Newcastle United.

'I didn't play in too many of the cup-ties at Newcastle, but I did play in some of them. In the First Division, I had some good games, such as Wolves away in the FA Cup – played well, won well. I think that they were all exciting games because they were all nervous games. I was always followed by that kind of nervousness that I talked about.

'We were playing Blackpool at Bloomfield Road and at that time, we had Alf McMichael at my left full-back for Newcastle United and Stanley Matthews was their outside-right. Little Ernie Taylor was the inside-right. Jimmy Armfield, the

England captain, was the right full-back. Charlie Mitten had said to me "You'll have to watch Jimmy Armfield," because he was one of the first players to start the overlapping of the full-back. In other words, the right-back was going past the outside-right who was slipping balls through for him. The right-back was meant to do a lot of the damage.

'Well, Stanley Matthews, being the player that he was, always insisted on having the ball at his feet. He would never run for a ball. Very seldom would he run for a through ball because he wanted it at his feet. Little Ernie Taylor was keeping on plying him. Before the game, Alf McMichael said to me "George, you'll have to keep coming back and keep an eye on Stanley Matthews, and I'll keep an eye on Jimmy Armfield if he's going to play this kind of game." So I did this.

'I was talking to Stanley Matthews for part of the time, because he tended to stand up on the touchline waiting for the ball coming to him, and they wouldn't give it to him because I was on him. What was happening was Jimmy Armfield was going past me and he was going past Alf McMichael. Little Ernie Taylor was slipping the ball in between Alf and me and he was doing all the damage. It got to a point basically, where Alf wanted me to chase the full-back, so we switched around and I kept an eye on Jimmy Armfield. So, instead of Jimmy Armfield marking me, it was me marking him for the full game.

'It went on like that. We tried to change it at half-time, but it kept happening. That was the start of the wing-backs of today. George Cohen, another England full-back, used to do the same thing. It always seemed to happen down the right-hand side, never the left for some reason. In history, you will find that Alf McMichael always played Stanley Matthews very well. In fact, it got to one point where Stanley Matthews said that he was not coming to St James' Park because he could never get anything out of Alf.

'I have to admit that Stanley Matthews never played many games at St James' Park. Whether or not it was because Alf used to play him very well, and he certainly did, I don't know. He played him off the park in international matches, because

Alf was very fast. He could keep up with him and he was good enough to get the tackles in.

'In those days, when they had the right and left-wingers coming back to tackle the outside-right or left, the full-back would then get the ball, just tap it forward, and say 'Go on George, just get yourself up there'. You were heaving for to get back, then he wanted you to turn round and sprint back to where you had just come from, while he was just standing around watching. So, we had one or two arguments about it, Alf and I, to be honest. It was just one of those things that we couldn't counteract for a while because of the overlapping full-back. If they got caught, they got hammered because you pulled the centre-half out of the way. When they were on the attack, they knew what they were doing. Of course, when you've got precision passes from the likes of Ernie Taylor, it wasn't easy to counteract it.'

When I asked George about his football idol, he chose a player who actually guested for Newcastle United during World War Two.

'My personal football hero was Tom Finney. For me, he was the complete footballer. He played outside-right for England and Preston North End and he was the master of the dribble. He could feint both ways with both feet and I know that George Best was good, but for me Tom Finney was better.

'Without a doubt, I think that the best centre-forward in the country, still today, is Alan Shearer. He impresses me very, very much as a footballer because he reads the game very well. He is excellent in the air. He has got to go down as being one of the best centre-forwards that Newcastle United have ever had. I would take him second to Jackie Milburn, but as far as a real true centre-forward, I think Alan Shearer is the best player at Newcastle today.'

George recalled his early memories of St James' Park and the Toon Army.

'When I first went there, it was absolutely vast. I used to go and train there as a schoolboy and in those days, we used to run around the cinder track. When I finished school, my schoolteacher used to take me to St James' Park and we used to go in there to train. We actually used to go onto the pitch and for me, just to put my feet on that grass at the age of 10 was just magic. The gymnasium up there was great. There were none of these training grounds like nowadays. We used to do all our training up there.

'We used to say that you could put 22 monkeys on the pitch at St James' Park and still get a crowd of 30,000. Newcastle still has a hard core of fans who will turn up whatever happens on the pitch. I think the Geordie public deserves better. The stadium now is absolutely magnificent. I have to take my hat off for what Sir John Hall has done for Newcastle United. He has done a tremendous job. He started it all off. The stadium is in the city in a cracking position. The town is buzzing on a Saturday when there's a home match.

'Don't forget though, when we were in the old First Division, we played in front of bigger crowds than they get now. It was standing room only and it was nothing to for us to get 50–55,000, especially if you had a cup tie. It didn't matter what the weather was like, it didn't make a difference, they were still there. It just seems to me now, running out at St James' Park, I would think that there was about 200,000 people inside. I know that there aren't really, but looking around, we had a certain stadium height when we played there. Nowadays the stands seem to go on forever.'

There was one occasion when the preparations for an away game had an unexpected element.

'When we used to play away at Manchester, we used to stay at the Queens Hotel. I think it was in Piccadilly, Manchester. I'll always remember this story. One of our players went to the toilet. We had come down for breakfast and he had gone off to the toilet. He was wearing braces and he took them off, pulled his trousers down, and sat on the toilet. What he hadn't realised was that his braces were dangling in the toilet. He did all his business on top of his braces. He came back after he had put them back on, not realising, and he sat down. There were a few of us sitting around and Ivor Allchurch said "By God, there's a funny smell knocking around here." He turned to the lad who had been to the toilet and said "By God, it's you man!" Well, he took his jacket off and his shirt was covered. He shouted "Oh my God, what's happened here?" I always remember that story. It was one of the daft kind of things that happened in those days.'

When comparing football in the 1950s to the present day, George shared his thoughts about the media, money, and managers.

'When you see some of the things in the papers today about football, there are a tremendous amount of things that go on between professional footballers and their managers. A reporter can only read between the lines. You don't get to know about some of the things. I'm so pleased for some players for the kind of money that the odd one gets. People think that all professional footballers are getting £15–17,000 a week. They're not, it's only the favoured few. Okay, I wouldn't go as far as to say that everybody playing in the Premiership isn't well paid, and quite rightly so. Why shouldn't they be? They are playing in front of 40–50,000 people.

'Why should it be just the directors of football clubs who are creaming off the money? When we played in front of

60,000 people, what happened to all that money? When you work out that players were getting £20 a week in those days, playing in front of an average 50,000 people, there was a tremendous amount of money went in. Where did it all go?

'I've always believed that a manager cannot tell you what to do when a ball is moving. In a game of football, hopefully the ball is moving most of the time. It is up to the individual player. Where a manager comes through, he is a motivator. He is an individual motivator. He is the kind of fellow who can come and talk to you and tell you your good points and your bad points. You can take those in and you can put those things right. But, when it comes down to team talks, you can do anything from a set ball. Anybody can do that. From a throw-in, a free-kick, a corner-kick, a goal-kick, you can all take up positions where a manager or yourselves decide. But, there are only those players on the field who can move around and move into positions when the ball is actually moving.

'I've always believed that if you go out onto the field as 11 pals, you will play better. Okay, you might say one or two things to each other, which they still do today, I'm sure, and it's forgotten about. You can call each other as much as you want on the field, but you are there to help each other.

'A good manager goes with a winning team and it is believed that a bad manager goes with a losing team. Someone like Bobby Robson will never be a bad manager, but if Newcastle United stayed at the bottom of the league until the end of a season, you couldn't say that he's a good manager. It's not the manager who is to blame in that case, it is the players. They are the ones who have really got to get together for to get to know each other's play.

'If you can get 11 pals on that pitch, that's the best thing. It's not easy to do at a football club. It's not easy to do at work.

35

To be honest, we had cliques. In football, you cannot expect everyone to get on together all the time. Some people read what is written in the papers and find that they are good players. Some of them believe it and take it to heart. Some don't and some remain normal. It doesn't matter what they read in the papers, they should just get on together. I would think that there are still cliques today and I know that we had them when I was at St James' Park.

'We used to meet for training, then go our separate ways. If you've got single lads in the team and married men with kids, you cannot expect them to live the same lifestyle. I'm sure that they don't, but there's still no reason why they cannot be good pals on the football field. I certainly never had any enemies at St James' Park.'

George Luke left Newcastle United in January 1961, transferring to Darlington, where he was able to rediscover his form, albeit at a lower level. Although he did not, by his own admission, achieve his true potential at Newcastle, it should not be forgotten that he faced the tasks of dislodging recognised internationals, experiencing the pain of relegation, and coping with serious injury during his career. George stayed loyal to his roots, playing all his football in the region. He served his time well and can proudly recall playing for his home club when it was indeed standing room only.

Chapter 3

BOBBY CUMMINGS
(1954–56, 1963–65)

ROBERT Douglas Cummings was born in Ashington on 17 November 1935. He first signed for Newcastle United as a youngster in May 1954, but at the time he didn't impress. He transferred to Ashington in November 1956, subsequently proving to be a prolific goalscorer, and was later signed by Aberdeen in 1960. Bobby was signed by Newcastle United for a second time in October 1963 for £5,000. Playing as a centre-forward, Bobby made 44 senior starts for Newcastle and he scored 14 goals.

Bobby was the kind of player who thoroughly enjoyed all aspects of football.

'I used to enjoy my training. I was always one of the last lads to finish. I always believed in training hard. We just did the sprints on a Friday. We didn't have that many real games of football, with kicking and passing of the ball. Lads were doing this and doing that, but there weren't many games. The boss, Joe Harvey, was great. He always got us to do what he wanted us to do.

'Some of the lads trained in the car park. It was a big slope and the goals were where the steps were. It was good, like, but you learned to be clever. But then we moved further down the road to the training ground. Once or twice we had to go across to Gateshead, not Gateshead's football ground, but another place over there, and we used to train over there. That was when we had the matches because there were proper goalposts. I don't know whose ground it was, but the manager wanted us to play 11-a-side and to get stuck in. I enjoyed that.

'Joe Harvey, the manager, would be watching you and if you didn't do as you were told, he would tell you. But he got the best out of most people. Luckily, when we won the league, I wouldn't say that we had the greatest team in the world, but we had a good side and everyone gave one hundred percent. We worked hard and at the finish, we were still gannin'. I found that all the lads really worked hard. They really gave their best all the time.'

Professional footballers today can earn vast sums of money compared to the players in the 1950s and 1960s. Today they will quite often live in large, detached houses located in exclusive areas, and they will drive to the training grounds and stadiums in their brand-new cars. Bobby's memories of the build-up to a home game at St James' Park show how much things have changed.

'It was funny, I had to travel from Blyth. I had a car for a spell, but I just got the bus up from Blyth to Newcastle. We had to go to the County Hotel before the games. We had a meal there, but I think there were only three things, certain things that you could have. Fish was one of them, and steak was another. It was alright, like. We used to walk up to the ground after the meal. Sometimes there was a bus laid on, but normally we would walk up to St James' Park. It wasn't very far, really. They wouldn't do it nowadays. We had to meet there and we'd talk about the game, you know, what was going to happen. That was about twelve o'clock, before we had our meal.'

One common criticism of footballers today is that they are distanced from the supporters. Some of the distance is generated by security, but some of it can sadly be the result of a degree of aloofness. The situation was quite different during the 1960s. Bobby had fond memories of the Newcastle United supporters and he shared a close relationship with some of them long after the final whistle had been blown.

'When we were there, it was different than today, because the people were that close together. When we played against Manchester United in the First Division and we got beat 2–1, when they had Denis Law and all the best players, the crowd was about fifty odd thousand. The atmosphere was just fantastic. Once you got into the ground, your mind was just on the football. You would look around and see all the people and you always knew that the ground was almost full. You would look to the left and see that the Leazes End had filled up.

'They were good supporters. They were fanatics, most of them. I thought that they were very good. I remember after games, I used to get the bus home. I got the number 6 bus all the time and there would be people on the way back who had been to the game, and they would crack on all the time. They weren't close to you, but they would just come up and talk to you. Young Ron Guthrie, who also played for Newcastle United, was on the same bus as well sometimes because he lived at Burradon. Sometimes people would want to buy you a beer, you know, things like that. It could cause a few problems. If you didn't want any more beer, sometimes you had to have one. You couldn't refuse. It was funny, really. In the pub back in Blyth, they would come up and talk to you. Like all Geordies, they loved their team.'

Newcastle United were promoted to the First Division at the end of the 1964/65 season. Bobby's most memorable performance came after he was established in the first team during the run-up to promotion.

'I can remember, we had played a draw, then we lost twice, then Joe Harvey changed the team. He dropped some of the lads and he put me in the team along with Bryan 'Pop' Robson. We were near the top of the league, playing away at Pompey [Portsmouth] and we had to win the game. There were 10 games to go. Joe put me and Pop in the team and from then on, we never lost a game. We didn't lose one game. In that game, when Joe changed the team, Pop and I both scored against Pompey. I'll always remember, half of the ground was covered with snow and the other half was clear. The stand on one side had kept the sun off the ground. I

think that my best performance was when we beat Pompey in that important game.'

Bobby scored 14 goals for Newcastle United. I asked him to recall his favourite and he chose one from a pre-season tour.

'I think that it was abroad. After we won the league in 1965, we went over to Denmark and Germany. I used to take the penalties when we were on tour and I remember that big John McGrath wanted to take one. Well, we were given one and John missed it. That was the end of that. Anyway, I remember in that game that someone had hit the ball and it went right in the bottom corner. I got there before any of the other lads and as I was coming in, about 40 yards from the goal, I saw that the keeper was coming out. I hit the ball and it swerved right into the top corner. I had just seen the keeper coming out and I just hit it.

'I think that we only played five or six games on tour and I scored five goals, as it happened. I scored two goals in Denmark and the others in Germany. We enjoyed ourselves on tour. I scored three goals against Rangers when I was with Aberdeen. I was the only Englishman to do that in the Scottish League at that time. I made my debut for Aberdeen against Arbroath in the Cup. I remember one game was snowed off, so I was asked to play for the Reserves. We played against Rangers Reserves. I was known as "The Englishman". I played against Rangers seven or eight times and I scored seven or eight goals.'

'My next game was against Rangers at Ibrox and it was a 2–2 draw. England were playing against Scotland a day or two later and Walter Winterburn was the manager then. We were staying in the same hotel and he just came over and said "Well done. Just stick in there". I think that was in 1959 or 1960.'

Bobby was a centre-forward and to him, playing against tough defenders was just part of the game. He actually suffered a broken leg on two occasions, but he just waited to recover, then he played on.

'Centre-halves wouldn't like it because I played hard. They stand off too much nowadays. I would never stand off anybody. When I played in a game, I wouldn't give anybody any room. I was taught to be up with them. You would never give a lad any room. If that ball is hit from 20 or 30 yards, by the time it gets there, you can nip in. If you didn't get the ball, you could tackle the lad. If you were clever enough, you could get there first and nick it away. It might have meant the difference of a goal.'

Bobby was a centre-forward, but at just under six foot, he was not that tall for his position. It was inevitable that some comparison with the modern-day strikers was made.

'I don't know if I am as tall as Alan Shearer, but I had the knack of jumping higher than all the big lads. I used to jump a fraction earlier. It's something that you do. You jump first. I used the ball with my head and my feet. I was taught to do it right.'

As highlighted earlier, Bobby received more than his fair share of knocks when trying to get the better of defenders. He recalled one occasion when he was summoned from his workplace to face a legend. It proved to be a somewhat painful experience.

'I was called out of the pit one day to play for the Reserves. I think that it was in 1955 or 1956. Newcastle United were at Leeds and the late John Charles was playing. We lost 7–4 and I scored three goals that day. Aye, I played against big John, but he was a gentleman. He kicked me in the head once when we played against Cardiff at Cardiff. His brother Mel was playing as well as John, but he was playing in defence.

'I remember when he kicked me. I knew that I was going to get the ball and I ran and dived for it. John was coming in the other way and he went to kick the ball. Well, we collided and he kicked me as well. I knew that I was going to get the ball, but he got me and I didn't know anything about it. I was injured but he was a proper gentleman. He came into the dressing room after the game and we had a bit of a crack. He was a monster of a man, you know. He kept saying "I wished you'd headed that ball, Bobby."

'I knew what it would be like playing as a centre-forward. Some defenders kicked you, but you had to kick back. If you kicked back, they respected you. They would say "This bugger kicks back, we'll have to watch what we're doing". Some of the Scottish lads were like that.'

When Bobby started supporting Newcastle United, there was only one hero for him.

'I would think that it was Jackie Milburn. I was about 12 when I started going to watch matches at St James' Park with my dad. Jackie was playing and so was Tommy Pearson. They had a good side then. I remember watching one game when Bobby Mitchell scored a couple of goals. We were getting beat. When the flag was taken down, there used to be 10 minutes to go. They took the flag down and suddenly Bobby scored. Someone else then scored and we finished up winning four something. Jackie Milburn was marvellous. He could pull the ball around all over the place. He was strong with both feet. He wasn't the best header of the ball. He gave you that lift all the time. He always knew when something could happen.

'When I was a lad and for years after that, they always used to pull the flag down with 10 minutes to go. I was always on the 'Popular' side at St James' Park. There was a café and you always used to go out there to go home. I used to say "Keep a seat for me". There were some great times, but I remember seeing Newcastle get beat 5–1 off Huddersfield and the bloke that was in goal for them was from Blyth!'

Youngsters who are discovered nowadays are generally spotted by scouts. Bobby first came to the attention of Newcastle United in a somewhat different way.

'I used to live in Blyth and we had a hut near the houses. I used to keep hitting the ball off this hut, which we used as our goal. Unknown to me, Benny Craig, who used to play for Newcastle United, was courting the lass next-door and he had seen me playing football. He actually married the lass who lived next-door. Well, Benny was in charge of the reserve team when I joined Newcastle and he knew that I was good at football because he had seen me kicking the ball. He was the first one to see me play. He played hard and if you didn't do as you were told, he would drop you.'

Bobby was full of admiration for the manager Joe Harvey and he recalled that the time before kick-off was generally a nervous moment.

'Joe was the best. He got you excited before you got on the field. Before we went out, we were all busy going to the toilet. Once you got out there, once you had gone down the tunnel, and you had seen all the people, you just wanted to kick the ball. You could get some terrible grounds, wet as anything. When we played against Sunderland, it was supposed to be cancelled, but it wasn't. There were 29,000 at the game and we beat them 1–0. I was playing against big Charlie Hurley. We won by a penalty that Ron McGarry scored. That was the only time that I played against Sunderland.'

Footballers in the modern game are in a position whereby they can earn well from playing and from endorsements. There is little doubt that, although it is time-limited, a career in football can be extremely lucrative for those players who are successful. Bobby feels that the money in football today has changed the game. He also highlighted inconsistencies in the modern game.

'That's all they think about today, the money. Maybe not all of them, but some players get that much money. They don't put their heart and soul into the game like the lads did in our day. You cannot tackle nowadays. They hardly do. If they do and they put their feet up, it's wrong. Some of them get away with it, some don't. The referees don't apply the same rules to everybody.'

Bobby left Newcastle United in October 1965. He moved on to Darlington where he played a crucial role in helping them achieve promotion. He later moved on to Hartlepool United in March 1968 and again he experienced promotion.

Bobby Cummings was a hard-working, local lad who loved playing football. He was regarded as one of the lads in his local community in Blyth, even though he played for Newcastle United. Bobby trained hard and he played hard, and even when he left St James' Park, he was still gannin'.

Chapter 4

BOBBY MONCUR
(1960–74)

ROBERT Moncur was born in Perth, Scotland, on 19 January 1945. He signed as an apprentice with Newcastle United in 1960 and signed professional in 1962. Bobby made 358 senior starts for Newcastle and scored 10 goals. He was a winner of the FA Youth Cup in 1962 and captained the team that won the Inter Cities Fairs Cup in 1969. He also won 16 full international caps playing for Scotland. Bobby commenced his football career with Newcastle United after moving south of the border at the age of 15.

'I moved to Newcastle when I was 15 years of age. I'd just been playing for Scottish Schoolboys. I'd been captain of them and I had the chance to go to a few places, Rangers, Hearts, Hibs, and I came down to England for trials with Burnley, Preston North End, Wolves, Manchester United and Newcastle United, to name but a few. Having gone round them all, as you do as a young kid, I decided on Newcastle, because I didn't want to stay in Scotland, as you couldn't become a professional until you were 17. This would have meant I had two years to get some sort of job, and I wanted to be a footballer.

'England had the apprenticeship scheme which you started at 15. Really, logically, I decided on Newcastle because it was just over the border. It was the best thing for me, because at 15 years of age, it was a big step going away from home, and Newcastle was just two and a half hours away. So, that was the start of it. I had a bit of a disaster, they put me in lodgings down at Whitley Bay. Logically, I couldn't walk between there and the ground, I had to get a train. I had to be at the ground for say nine o'clock in the morning to work all day. So, I decided very quickly to move and I went into digs in Stamfordham Road. That settled me down a bit.'

Bobby's move away from home as a teenager got off to an unsettled start, but he benefited greatly from some good support and some influential comments from his father.

'I was very lucky at the time that one of the coaches at Newcastle, Alan Thompson, really took me under his wing. I'm very grateful to Alan after all these years. But for him, the homesickness might have come into it. Alan used to take me golfing on a Sunday. That was a very lonely day if you'd played on the Saturday and don't forget, at that stage at 15 years of age, you're wondering if you're going to make the grade. So, there was pressure on me because I didn't want to go back a failure.

'When you had a bad game and things weren't going too well, it was very easy to say, I'm going home. I used to get on the phone to my father and tell him that I wasn't happy. He was great, he used to talk me into it. He would say "Look, just give it another week, give it another fortnight, and if you still feel the same way, you can come home, no problem". Then he added "Mind, you will be coming home a failure". As it turned out, he was right, as always. As things went on, things were better. As I say, in the early days, Alan Thompson was great for me. It was a good time for me, I really enjoyed it. Then Joe Harvey came, of course.'

I asked Bobby why he had chosen to pursue a career in football.

'That's an easy one, because I was good at it. I think I was better at that than some other sports, albeit I was quite handy at a lot of things. There weren't many sports, although at 17 years of age, I had become a decent golfer as well. My dad gave me a proper set of golf clubs when I signed on for Newcastle, when I was 15, which was a great present because it allowed me to go and play golf, which I have to say was very important to me.'

Bobby almost didn't become a professional footballer, but fortunately for Newcastle United, his childhood experience gave him strength to see it through.

'At one stage I had given up football because when I was a young kid, where I stayed at, I played for the county team. I went to a school seven or eight miles away and I had to travel by bus, sometimes two buses, to get there. I had to leave the school and go another 14 miles away to train on a Tuesday and a Thursday night and then go all the way back to my village. I wasn't getting home until half past eleven at night, and I had to carry all the training gear. It was a tough old time for me. I earned whatever I got, I'll tell you, by doing these bus trips. I was half-asleep, well I was knackered by the time I got home. I learned to stand on my own two feet.'

Before moving to Newcastle, Bobby's football idols came from local clubs.

'In my time, Hibs had a team which included the 'Famous Five'. There was Gordon Smith, Lawrie Reilly, Bobby Johnson, Willie Ormond, and someone else whose name escapes me. They were the 'Famous Five' and I suppose I saw the latter end of them. Lawrie Reilly was called 'Last Man Reilly' because he scored goals at the end of the game. So, Hibs were very much my team, but so were Hearts because at that time I was so keen to go and watch football matches. When anybody asked which team did I support, I used to watch both sides because I was just interested in football. I never supported Rangers or Celtic, it was always Hibs or Hearts. I was born in Perth, so St Johnstone was close to my heart as well.'

Bobby's early experiences of training did not quite match his expectations.

'Well, I was an apprentice and our day was typically, you would come in at nine o'clock in the morning and you would get all the gear ready for the pros coming in. I remember once there were 64 professional footballers and all their gear. The night before, you'd dry all the gear. You had to look after players. You were their man, almost like a prefect. You would go and get their gear, get their boots organised, and do fairly mediocre tasks in terms of looking after pros.

'Then we might go and train. We didn't always train, because if the terraces needed sweeping, on a Monday or Tuesday after a Saturday match, that got the priority, which I was always fed up about. You were there to play football, not sweep terraces. I wouldn't say it was slave labour, that's probably the wrong words, but we weren't being trained to be professional footballers. But, as the week went on, once they'd run out of jobs for us to do, then we got our training. There were 15 of us then, all apprentices, and we would all sweep the terraces together. We used to have a lark and have some good laughs. We used to dodge away from the groundsman. He used to drive around trying to catch us, but he had a problem, we were quicker than he was.

'So, that was my initial thing. Then the game on the Saturday of course was the highlight. During the week, it was enjoyable because there were 15 of us. But the hard part was actually doing things that you didn't believe you should have been doing. That was done away with. It's a different ball game nowadays.'

Although Bobby became an accomplished centre-half, he experienced playing in a number of different positions.

'I started off as a left-half, but in the Youth Cup team. I played left-back for Scottish Schoolboys initially because I was one of the smallest. Over the period of junior trials, I finished up as big as any of them and then I got the job of centre-half and captain. When Charlie Mitten brought me down to Newcastle, I made my debut for Newcastle United at West Wylam and I scored six at inside-left. I wasn't bad with my left foot, but I was a right-footed player who worked so hard with my left.

'They played me two or three times in that position. In fact, we won the FA Youth Cup and I was inside-left. In the old

days, I usually say this, I used to do all Alan Suddick's work for him and he used to get the headlines. That was the way it was in those days. I didn't mind that because he was a great talented player.

'Then I was struggling a little bit there and they moved me back to left-half and that's where I played for a couple of years. Eventually, when I made my debut for the first team, I actually made it at centre-half, alongside Jim Iley. In the promotion year, 1965, I was just filling in for John McGrath, Jim Iley, Stan Anderson, if they got injured, and that season I played 11 games in the promotion side. The following year, a similar thing happened, I played 20-odd games. After that, when Jim Iley left, I was established in the team.'

During his early playing career at Newcastle, Bobby was, not surprisingly, keen to be in the first team. His frustration at not being there led to a transfer request, with an unexpected outcome.

'I actually went and asked Joe Harvey for a move. I said "Look, I think I'm good enough to be playing in the First Division". He didn't disagree. I was thinking of getting married as well. I wanted to be playing full-time. I didn't want to be hanging around for John McGrath, Jim Iley, or whoever. Joe, in his wisdom, said "I'll put you on the list". He asked me "What do you think is a fair price?" As it turned out, we agreed on £25,000. Bryan 'Pop' Robson, at the same time, was in a similar situation.

'£25,000 they put on me and I kept reading in the papers that John Gibson from the *Chronicle* was saying Norwich were definitely in for me. I kept reading this in the papers, so I thought that it must have been true. Joe kept saying "They won't pay the money". After about a month I eventually got in the first team and stayed in there. It was all these years later when I was skipper that I asked Joe "What happened with Norwich?" He said "Look, son, you were going nowhere". The truth was that Joe kept putting up the price every time Norwich came in for me. That was Joe's clever management. He realised then that I was probably going to do a good job for him.'

Bobby got on well with manager Joe Harvey, who was to prove equally adept at passing on certain responsibilities.

'I remember when I was skipper, if we didn't have a very good result on the Saturday, you'd read the papers on the Sunday. I'd go in and train on the Monday morning. He would send someone in to say "You'd better go on Tyne Tees Television tonight Bobby, to talk about that bloody disaster on Saturday". So, I'd go down and walk in and say "It's Bobby Moncur for George Taylor" and they would say "Oh, what's the matter, can Mr Harvey not make it?" Joe was clever at these little tricks. He used to send me on the s****y jobs. He didn't like going on the telly. He was very good, but he didn't like it. I had a great relationship with him.'

The highlight of Bobby's Newcastle United career was the European adventure that resulted in victory in the Inter Cities Fairs Cup Final in 1969.

'People always say "You were lucky, you went in the back door". I say "Yeah, but we walked out the front". That's my thinking about it. We did go in the back door, but that was the rules and the regulations. We didn't cheat, we got in there, rightly so, because of the regulations, and the fact that we got in that way, we had a good team spirit at the time. The team was just starting to become a unit. Joe was good at buying players. He was good at buying the odd character. He was clever at building the team. He did it twice in my lifetime, once in 1969 and then in 1974.

'The team that we won the Fairs Cup with in 1969 was the best team I ever played in. When I say team, I mean team spirit. When we were on that pitch, there was nobody who didn't pull their weight. People had different qualities. You read nowadays about splits in the camp. Well, there's a split in every camp. You can't tell me, when you've got 14 guys, that they all do the same things. They don't all play golf. There was Wyn Davies, Tommy Gibb, who used to like to go to the races. There was Willie McFaul, Pop, David Craig, and myself, we were all more into the golfing side. If you like, there were two sides of it, but there was never any animosity. On that pitch, whenever you put on that shirt, everybody was all for one and one for all.

'It was just such a great team spirit. That's what won us the Fairs Cup. The fact that we'd got to play all these great sides, they were just like names to us. We beat some good sides. Luckily enough, most of the games we played away first. I always said that if we came out of this 2–0 down, we would still win it at home. I was only 24 at the time, the second youngest player in the team. Even though I was skipper, I was the second youngest. At the time, being a young lad, it was all exciting and you never really took in all you should've done. When I look back, I think what a wonderful experience that must have been. But I can't remember too much about it apart from the final itself.

'Two things I remember, one is after we won and I was presented with the cup, we were running round the pitch. I remember someone jumping on my back. I turned round ready to hit whoever it was. It was my wife. She had run onto the pitch and jumped on my back and I didn't know who the hell it was. When someone jumps on your back, you panic, don't you?

'The other memory is Joe Harvey, who was a master man-manager. I was never ever sure about his tactical nous, in as much as his typical team talk was "Get out there, get stuck in". If we asked him technical questions, that was it. He'd been out there three to four weeks before with all the press boys. They used to go away for three to four days. God knows what they did. But, one thing they didn't do was tell us once about the team. I think it was a jolly. So, when we asked him, Joe was very reluctant to tell us about half of the players. I don't think he knew half the names anyway.

'His greatest tactical team talk was in the Fairs Cup Final over there. We had beaten them 3–0 at St James'. We had a good back four then. The whole of Tyneside said we were going to win the cup, myself included. Anyway, we went out there and don't forget, Ujpest Dozsa had been described by Don Revie as the best club he'd ever seen. Of course, we beat them at home, so we were thinking, they cannot be that good.

'Anyway, before the game started, you had to toss a coin with the other skipper to decide who went out and warmed up first, like they do now or similar. Whoever won the toss had the choice to warm up first or second, because you warmed up separately. We were out first, so some 40 minutes before the game started, we were out for 10 or 15 minutes. I remember going out there, it was 9 June and it was a real hot, balmy night, really oppressive in terms of trying to run about. So, after about 10 minutes, we'd had enough and we walked back to the dressing room. Even by that time, our kit was wet with sweating.

'So, we're sitting thinking we'd have to make the ball do all the work, all that stuff. Joe says "Right, I'll go and see what the enemy's like". So off he goes, cigarette in his mouth as always. Coming back about four minutes later, he says "Bloody hell, have we got problems tonight. This is a far different team to the one you played in Newcastle. They're bombing around everywhere, knocking 50, 60-yard balls. They're like bloody rabbits, they're all over the place. You've got a big job on tonight, boys, and it won't be easy, but get out there. Good luck". Then he left us. That was his team talk.

'Half-time came, of course we were getting stuffed, weren't we? It could've been 6–0. They were hitting the post, hitting the bar. Willie was having a blinder. We were defending like mad and at half-time it was 2–0, it could've been a lot more. So we trooped into the dressing room. I was sitting with my head in my hands and the sweat was forming a pool on the floor. We were all the same, heads down, absolutely gutted, thinking we were going to lose it. You think about all the people back home.

'So, we're sitting there, absolutely devastated, no sign of the gaffer, and there was very little said. Then, bursting through the door, there's Joe. He looks round the dressing room and says "What's the problem?" Nobody answered. Then he says "Come on, what's the problem?" So, being skipper, I said "What's the problem, Gaffer? We're getting stuffed and we don't know what to do about it. We've no chance, we cannot stop them. They're just far better on the ball." "Alright", he says, "there is no problem. All you've got to do is go out there and score a goal. These foreigners will collapse like a pack of cards, I'm telling you. Get out there and score a goal and that'll be it". He walked out. That was his team talk at half-time. There was nothing about tactics. He just walked out of the dressing room and he was gone.

'As history will tell you, I went up for a corner, the ball went back out again to Sinclair, came back in, I hooked it in the back of the net. From there, the rest is history. So, after all the celebrations, running round the pitch, and all the rest of it, we'd got this big long cup in the dressing room. There was still no sign of Joe. The champagne was flowing. I said "Where's the gaffer?" Five minutes later, the door bursts open, it's the gaffer. He walked in, stood there, his hands in the air, cigarette, and he says "What did I ******* tell you?" To this day I don't know whether that was brilliant management or good luck. Who knows?'

Bobby rated his performance as a young player against Manchester United as his best on an individual basis.

'I actually played at Old Trafford in my early days. I was only a kid at the time. I think I was deputising for John McGrath and I actually played in a youth team match down in London the night before. I travelled up by sleeper from London, then I caught the bus or the train down to Manchester and played that night at Old Trafford. There was a guy called Ken McKenzie who gave merit marks in the *Journal*. He gave Gordon Marshall 10+ and I think he gave me 10. It was my early days as centre-half. We actually drew that night, which was a good result for us. That was a good performance, coming in as a young kid. I think after that I never looked back.

'I was only about six feet, I was never massive. People always think I was good in the air, but I wasn't that tall. I remember playing against Denis Law and Bobby Charlton, thinking to myself, that centre-halves always feel they've got to be the commander. So I was a little bit apprehensive, but as a young kid you just go out there and do it.'

Bobby scored 10 goals for Newcastle United. He actually scored an 11th goal against Nottingham Forest in a contro-versial cup tie that was ordered to be replayed following a pitch invasion. He rated his early second-half goal in the

Inter Cities Fairs Cup Final second leg against Ujpest Dozsa as his favourite.

'Probably the best goal, something I'd been trying to do for years, was the goal I scored over in Budapest because that changed the match. I say to myself, it was a fantastic strike. I was at the corner of the six-yard box to the left of the goal. We went up there very quickly after the start of the second half, the ball came in from a corner, it was knocked back out to Jackie Sinclair and he hit it back in. It was actually going behind me and I remember I had to get behind it with my left foot to still hook it into the net. When you hit it right, like in golf, you know you've hit it right, and it went in like a bullet. I remember a guy trying to stop it with his hand and it just knocked him out of the way.

'To me technically it was something I was good at doing. I was good at getting my body round, sticking the ball in the back of the net. I think that was my best goal, the best strike anyway. I think even Alan Shearer would've been proud of that one. So, that was just a volley, well in the air, and I just whacked it.

'I was always lucky when I scored a goal, they were usually very important. I scored the winner in the FA Youth Cup Final. I scored the winner in the Texaco Cup Final, that was a cracking goal, probably better than the other one. That was another volley from outside the box from about 30 yards. The Inter Milan goal, which caused a riot when their 'keeper was sent off, that wasn't a bad goal, with me coming off the line and heading it in. It wasn't a great goal, but it was a good goal because it was so important to us.'

Playing as a centre-half, Bobby faced some formidable opponents.

'When I was younger, obviously Greavsie [Jimmy Greaves] when I was playing left-half. He was always a nightmare,

59

because he was such a clinical finisher. He used to chat away all the game to take your attention away, then all of a sudden he'd be off, steal a yard on you, and you were 1–0 down.

'I didn't like playing against little guys. The big guys, rough tough blokes, I didn't have a problem with because I could match them. It was just that I didn't like guys who were quick, could go both ways. When you've got George Best coming at you, it was a bit of a nightmare. I felt that I actually did well against him. I don't know how, but I managed to always contain him quite well. In fact, he got sent off against me in a home international match, when he threw the mud at the referee.

'When people say I played left-half or centre-half, I was never an out-and-out sweeper. I was always the more defensive of the central two. Most of my career I played alongside John McNamee and Ollie Burton. David Craig and Frank Clark were invariably the full-backs. We used to play two on two in the middle. So, I was a central defender, but not a sweeper. I still had to mark my man.'

Robert Rutherford was a director of Newcastle United, who ultimately became chairman. He was also a surgeon, like his father before him. He was the central figure in one of Bobby's more memorable stories.

'Bob Rutherford, who was club chairman, was also the club surgeon. When I got my cartilage done in 1968, Bob used to operate down at South Shields General. I knew Bob quite well because I was skipper as well and he was a good golfer, and I wasn't bad as well. He was a real man's man. I got on well with him. In those days, you had to go in the night before your operation. My knee had actually locked in a pre-season friendly against a Hibs-Hearts Select. My mother never used to come and watch me play, very rarely, because she always worried that I would get hurt. Twice she came to see me play and twice I got injured, so that was it. I got carried off at Easter Road.

'To cut a long story short, they couldn't free my leg, so Bob came up on the Sunday and said "Right, I'll operate on Tuesday". So, I go in and they shaved me from top to bottom, which I never did understand. About an hour before, they give you a pre-med injection, which is supposed to relax you. I got this injection and it had this effect on me, which I didn't think so at the time. As they wheeled me along on this trolley thing, I'm chatting away to everyone. I'm saying "I'm not sure that thing's worked". Anyway, they wheeled me in backwards, as they do. I'm claustrophobic, I hate anything over my face and I told them I didn't want any mask on. I knew there'd be a mask going on, but I didn't want to be awake when it happened.

'So, they wheeled me in backwards and everyone wore green gowns with a mask over their faces. The anaesthetist came in and said "Right Bob, I'm going to give you a jab". I said "Where's Mr Rutherford?" He says "Oh, he's around somewhere. I want you to count to thirty. You won't make it".

'I'm lying there thinking, you really think so? I go "One, two, three, four, five, six, seven… " and I'm starting to go. All of a sudden, this great big shadow came from behind me, stood at the end of my feet and went "It is your left leg, isn't it Bob?" I woke up thinking, bloody hell he's done the wrong leg. He got his own back for all the mickey-taking.'

Newcastle United's victory in the Inter Cities Fairs Cup in 1969 brought the last major trophy to St James' Park. Expectations of further major silverware have been high ever since and yet, after 35 years, the trophy cabinet still beckons. Bobby Moncur, captain of that successful team, eventually moved on in 1974 after 14 years service to Newcastle United. He went in the back door as a 15-year-old boy and walked out of the front door as a very successful man. I am sure that his proud father was delighted that Bobby did not return home a failure.

Chapter 5

DAVE HILLEY
(1962–67)

DAVID Hilley was born in Glasgow on 20 December 1938. He signed for Newcastle United from Third Lanark in Scotland in August 1962 in a £40,000 deal that included goalkeeper Stewart Mitchell. Dave was an inside-forward who was seen as a replacement for Ivor Allchurch. He made 209 senior appearances for Newcastle United and scored 33 goals. My first question to

Dave was what he thought he would have been valued at today if he were playing professional football in the Premiership.

'It's very difficult to work out, really. I would probably be valued at seven million against today's prices, not your 10 or 15 million.'

Dave played for Newcastle United in the 1960s when life at St James' Park was somewhat different from today. I asked Dave to recall what it was like at that time.

'It's like night and day. The conditions when we played there were very poor. When you talk about the changing facilities, the press box, and the actual facilities for the fans, they were virtually non-existent in those days. It was a matter of getting as many fans as you could into the ground. The supporters stood cheek to jowl. Even the pitch wasn't particularly good.

'That's one of the things that I think about a lot, the playing surfaces now compared to when we played. We would play at Derby County in six inches of mud and often that was the opening game of the season. The pitch was just a quagmire. The quality of football today has a lot to do with the quality of the pitches. So, the facilities were pretty basic.'

Dave's personal recollections of the training facilities at Newcastle United perhaps help to illustrate how much things have changed nowadays. He also reflected on the differences between his playing days and the modern game.

'Again, the training facilities were extremely basic. We trained at Hunters Moor. So we would report to St James' Park in the morning, get changed there, then we would jog up Barrack Road. All we had there was one pitch and a big wooden shed. There were no toilet facilities or showers or anything. It was very basic. It was like a pub team. Newcastle in those days were not a very professionally run outfit compared to some of the big clubs at the time. They were a family-run club for many years during that era and it was run like that instead of a football club for the local fans.

'When you compare it to the modern game, I can hardly ever remember many injuries to be honest, unless it was a broken leg. I cannot understand things like the pulled muscles that they have nowadays. It's got to be remembered that, in our day, defenders tackled from behind, yet the injuries were minimal compared to what they are today. Now, people say that it's because the game is much quicker. Certainly, the players are much fitter and stronger and they train a lot better, but I can't understand the number of injuries that players get today.

'There is possibly another reason as well. We had small squads in our time. If you had 15 or 16 players in the senior squad, that was about it, and you felt that you had to play every week. Very often, you would play when you were not 100 percent fit. Occasionally you would have a cortisone injection and you just went out and played. The players today won't do that. Clubs today wouldn't do that. Their players are too valuable. Also a lot of players today have massive contracts and they perhaps don't want to take a chance. They will say if they don't feel fully fit. They have big squads today that can cover that. In our day, they hadn't. You played the same team every week if they were there.'

Although Dave scored several goals for Newcastle United, he recalled that his most memorable performance was in a game when his name did not actually appear on the scoresheet.

'Strangely enough, it was a game at Coventry when I didn't actually score a goal. It was a cup tie and I was playing on the left wing. I'd been out of favour at the time and was brought back in. It was one of those games when everything went fantastically well for me. I laid on three goals for Wyn Davies that day. He got the hat-trick, but they were virtually tap-ins. That was definitely my best performance.

'I had another very good game against Middlesbrough in the 1964/65 season when we won promotion, winning the championship. We played them twice over the Christmas period. I scored once at Middlesbrough and we came back to St James' Park when we won 2–0 and I scored both goals. So that was also an important win.'

Dave scored 33 goals for Newcastle United. His choice of favourite goal actually came from a Tyne-Tees derby match.

'I think it was probably in the game against Middlesbrough. There was snow on the ground for both matches and I can vaguely remember picking up the ball midway into their half. I went on a bit of a mazy dribble and I think that I beat two or three players before slipping the ball past their 'keeper. I remember that one. I don't remember too many of them to be honest because I wasn't the kind of player to thrash them in from 35 yards. I was a maker rather than a taker of goals, but I do remember that one because it was a bit special.'

The highlight of Dave's Newcastle United career was a home match at Easter 1965.

'Probably winning the championship in 1965 because we played Bolton on Good Friday at St James' Park. We had to win that game to guarantee promotion, not to guarantee the championship, and it was a really emotional day. There were 59,960 in the ground. It was just phenomenal. The atmosphere was just incredible and the response from the crowd, the passion, and the emotion that day was very, very special.'

Dave played for Newcastle United for five years during 1962–67 and celebrated his first season in the First Division by being the team's only ever-present player during the 1965/66

season. It was not surprising that it was with some sadness that Dave's career at St James' Park came to an end.

'I was disappointed to leave Newcastle when I did, because the following season they won the Fairs Cup. I hadn't been getting a regular game and I was very surprised actually when someone contacted me and said "Nottingham are in for you". I thought that they were talking about Notts County and I was delighted to hear that it was Nottingham Forest, because the previous season they had been runners-up in the league and had been in the semi-final of the Cup. They had a really star-studded side at that time, but I had always played well against them. I remember that. They were short of players through injury and they came in for me as a utility player. I loved my time at Nottingham and I did really well there, and because of injuries, I actually played virtually two seasons regularly in the first team.'

Joe Harvey was the manager of Newcastle United throughout Dave's time with the club. Dave reflected on his influence.

'He was a terrific character. I was actually Joe's first signing. He wasn't a football coach, but he was a tremendous motivator. He had a couple of good coaches working with him when I was there, so he didn't have to coach the football team. He would come into the dressing room and wind the players up and then you went out there and played. He would have died for the club. That's the way that he felt about Newcastle United and he expected his players to do the same. Under Joe Harvey, there was tremendous team spirit in the dressing room and that carried them through in the Fairs Cup. They beat some quality sides. When he turned up at a practice match, everyone lifted their game by about 10 percent, just because he was standing at the side of the pitch, watching what was going on. He was a hard man, but fair.'

To the supporters of Newcastle United, there are no bigger games than those against arch-rivals Sunderland. Dave recalled playing in the Tyne-Wear derby matches.

'To be honest, I don't remember too much of the actual football in the derby matches. They were over in no time and were such frenzied games. When you played matches like that, it was half-time before you knew it. You would think that it was 20 minutes into the game and yet it was virtually gone. I do remember one particular game when Alan Suddick and myself linked up incredibly well on the day and we beat Sunderland 2–0 at St James' Park. Alan and I virtually destroyed them and we linked up perfectly that day. It came off for us and that was a special memory. We had beaten our local rivals, of course.'

The modern game of football is far more complex off the field, with the intricacies of contracts, endorsements and sponsorships, and of course the sometimes questionable activities of players' agents. Football has changed so much since Dave played and not always for the better. He reflected on the differences between the 1960s and the modern era.

'The biggest difference for me is the lack of loyalty of players towards their clubs nowadays. There are mercenaries travelling around the modern game. They come and sign big contracts, then give virtually nothing to the clubs. It is a tremendous loss. Another thing is that a number of players coming from abroad don't have the feel for the club in the same way that the local lads have, or the Scottish or Irish lads. When we came to Newcastle, you gave it everything that you had. To see these big stars now, floating around the game in England, the passion is not there. I think that maybe a bit of the passion has gone out of the derby matches because a lot of the foreign players don't quite understand what it is all about and how much it means to the fans.'

Looking back to his earlier years as a football supporter, Dave recalled his personal heroes.

'I was a Third Lanark supporter and that is the reason that I signed for them when I was about 18. I had chances to go to lots of other clubs: Celtic, Wolves, Sheffield, Everton and Newcastle, but I wanted to play for the club that I loved as a youngster. My hero at that time was an inside-forward, the number eight playing for Third Lanark, Jimmy Mason, who was a Scottish international. He was a fantastic player. He wasn't physically strong, but he had fantastic guile and ability and he was a lovely passer of the ball. He was just a joy to watch.

'So Jimmy Mason was my big hero, but also Bobby Mitchell. Bobby went to the same school as I went to and I used to watch him play juvenile football in a local park before he went into the Third Lanark side. So, Bobby was another hero of mine and I actually finished up living quite close to him when I signed for Newcastle. He had nearly stopped playing at that time. So they were my two heroes.'

I asked Dave if he thought that he could play in the present-day Newcastle United squad, were he currently in his prime.

'It's very difficult to equate that, because if I was playing today I would be much fitter and faster than I was 30 years ago. In terms of skill, there would be no doubts about it. I don't lack the skill of those playing today. I could certainly play in the Premiership. Yes, I'd be confident of that. Although having said that, they do bring in lots of players from abroad and that would make it more difficult for the home-grown players.

'Alan Shearer is the epitome of the perfect professional as far as I am concerned, although he is not the kind of player that I was. You couldn't find a better professional than Alan. What he has done for Newcastle United has been absolutely phenomenal and you just wonder what it is going to be like when he actually stops playing. His professionalism, his commitment to the game, his consistency, his willingness to take responsibility, he has got the lot.'

Dave compiles the match reports of Newcastle United's home games for the *Sunday Post* newspaper. I wondered if he kicked every ball when preparing his notes.

'I don't think about that at all. I can enjoy watching the game. People do get surprised when I don't get too passionate about it, but they forget that I am not actually a Newcastle United supporter. I was a Third Lanark supporter and I say to them "Look, you don't understand my lack of passion, but if your team had died, could you suddenly go and support another team with that same passion?" It just doesn't work that way. Of course, I played for Newcastle and I go and watch them play regularly, and I am desperately keen for them to do well. But, I'm not as passionate as your normal Geordie fans who go to watch the team, because it is their team.'

Supporters of Newcastle United have always loved their football, as Dave recalled.

'They have always been the same. I do a bit of after-dinner speaking and I was doing Wallsend Boys Club the other night, and I couldn't get away. Fans were coming up and were talking to me about the old days when they used to come and watch me play. Their passion just surprises you sometimes and their love for the club. The modern-day fans are exactly the same. The passion for the club has always been there and always will be there for the local people. It is absolutely phenomenal.

'Peter Lorimer, the former Leeds United player, was at the same dinner and he made the point that St James' Park is one of the few stadiums that you can regularly fill with 50,000 every home game and they are all local people. Manchester United can fill their ground, but they come from all over the country, and sometimes all over the world. For local passion for a team, I don't think that there is any club anywhere that can beat Newcastle.

'Another thing, the women in this city know a lot about the club and about football as well, which is quite incredible. You don't normally get that. It is not just because the husbands go to watch the team, it is because they are passionately involved in the local team as well. It is very unique.'

Footballers always relive their glory moments, but there is usually at least one moment that they would prefer to forget.

'Well, the most embarrassing moment was when I missed a goal. It must have been about two yards off the goal line. We were playing away at Grimsby and someone rolled the ball across, and just as I went to tap it in, the ball bobbled and it went over the top of the bar. That was really embarrassing. That was the only one that I can think of… although there were a few other ones that I missed. There is one thing about the Geordie fans, when you are doing well, they will let you know and they will be behind you. If you have a bad game, they will let you know that as well. It is because they are passionate about the game.

'I do remember one game that was very embarrassing. We actually went out of the FA Cup to a non-league team, Bedford Town. They beat us something like 2–1 at St James' Park. It took a lot of getting over and the fans reminded you a lot about that, because of the bad performance.

'There have been players who took quite a lot of stick from the fans. There have been odd players who have not won over the fans and have had to go very quickly. I must say that for most of the time I was there, I had a good relationship with the fans. It was a great experience.

'I actually played against Bobby Robson quite regularly in the 1960s, when he played for Fulham and West Brom. I played against him a few times for Newcastle. The job that he has done has been absolutely phenomenal.'

Dave Hilley played for Newcastle United for five years under manager Joe Harvey. On retiring from the game, he settled on Tyneside and continues to be involved in football through coaching and journalism. Dave regularly goes to St James' Park to watch Newcastle play and to write his match reports. Although he has explained how he can be more objective about the performances nowadays, I would perhaps be wary of sitting in front of him, just in case he decides to go on another mazy dribble.

Chapter 6

RON McGARRY
(1962–67)

RONALD James McGarry was born in Whitehaven, Cumbria on 5 December 1937. He signed for Newcastle United from Bolton Wanderers in December 1962 for £17,500. A strong centre-forward, Ron made 129 senior starts for Newcastle United and scored 46 goals. His route to signing for the Magpies could not have been described as orthodox, but then neither was his playing career. However, his footballing prowess proved to be an early advantage. I'll let Ron explain.

'I was in the Army and I played for the team. I was scoring 6, 10, 12 goals a game because the league we were in wasn't all that good. The more goals I scored, every time I was on guard, if I broke the record I got off guard duty on the Thursday night. So I kept breaking the records and I think I only did two guards all the time I was in the Army.

'Then I got a phone call from the commandant one day saying "Carlisle United have been on the phone asking for you to go down for a trial. I'll take you down in my car." So we get down to Carlisle and they'd just kicked off. We went in and I said who I was, and the manager says "Oh, we've just kicked off. Will you come back some other time?" When we left I said to the commandant "There's no way. I could've gone on at half time. They sent for me." So, I never bothered.

'A fortnight later, Joe Harvey was at one of the matches I was playing in for the Army and he said "Will you come to Workington for a trial on Thursday night?" I agreed and played in a cup final for the Army on the Thursday afternoon, then went down and played for Joe's reserves and I scored a goal. He signed me on straight away. Then I got a phone call from Whitehaven Rugby League Club asking me if I could go down for a trial with them. So I had a trial as a stand-off half and they wanted to sign me. At the time Workington were giving you more money for expenses than the rugby team. So, I signed amateur for Workington and that's how I got into football.

'When I was ready for leaving the Army, Joe Harvey signed me full-time for Workington Reds. That was in 1960. I had about 12 months there and Joe said "I'll be getting the Newcastle job and I'll buy you." Well, in the meantime,

Everton came in for me, then Bolton came in for me and that's where I went.

'I was at Bolton for about 12 to 14 months when I got a phone call from Joe telling me that a scout was coming down to watch me play, because he wanted to take me to Newcastle. The scout came down and watched me play, then the next week Joe came down to Bolton and signed me himself. That was the start of my career with Newcastle United.'

On moving to the north-east, Ron found life a little different to what he had been used to. Newcastle proved to be a bit of a culture shock compared to Bolton.

'When I arrived in Newcastle, all the lads were wearing brothel creepers and I couldn't understand a word they were saying. It was all divvn't this and divvn't that. Mind you, I loved every minute of it. Newcastle was a fantastic place to come to.

'When I first came to Newcastle, they were training at the White City ground over at Blaydon. It was just a field actually with a dog track round it. Then we moved up to Barrack Road, which wasn't much better. During the pre-season training we used to have to go right up round Gosforth, right round the Town Moor. You were going on a seven or eight-mile trek for a week before you even saw a ball.

'You were three days taking the blisters off your feet because we used to run with the big Army boots on to strengthen your legs. You never saw a ball. Joe Harvey used to say "Once you start the season, you'll see the ball and you'll want it more." That was our pre-season training. It was very, very hard, but we didn't get the injuries that you seem to get nowadays. If we got injured we were maybe off for a week or so, or a couple of weeks, but now they seem to be off for six months, some going into 12 months.

'I can't understand whether they're fitter now than we were. I don't know. I don't believe in going straight in and onto the ball in training from pre-season. I think you should be strengthened up first. Tone your muscles up with the weights or running. I know that we used to get hard tackles and all that, but you got up. You didn't go in intentionally to maim like some do today, we went for the ball.

'When you see them today, they might be sliding in for the ball and they trip someone over, and they're yellow carded. Then you see a bloke lashing out and still just gets a yellow card. He should get a red card. We had robust, strong tacklers, but you just got up and got on with it. Nowadays it seems like a totally different game altogether.'

All players have to prepare themselves for the matches and no two preparations are alike. Ron was always relaxed before kick-off.

'I had one of the funniest build-ups going. I used to go down town, nip into the betting shop at 12 o'clock, have a couple of bets, and then get myself to the ground for two o'clock. Then I used to lie down and have a massage on the legs. I would get my shorts on and that, and do a few exercises ready for going out. Now some of the lads would just go down for two o'clock. They didn't have to arrive any earlier because there was no meal. You had your meal at home, if you were going to have something to eat.

'You had to report in for two o'clock for a three o'clock kick-off, which gave you plenty of time to more or less get changed. Big John McGrath used to just come in at two o'clock to get changed. He never did any exercises. He used to just go out and play. The one thing about me was that I was always relaxed. It really didn't bother me. To me it was a job like someone going into a factory. I was going there to do a job the best that I could for 90 minutes, and then that was me finished.'

Ron was one of football's true characters and certainly attracted a lot of publicity.

'I was playing at Swansea and I got sent off. Their centre-half and I had been knocking each other all the time and he had been chopping me every time I went through. So we got into a fight and we had a slogging match on the field, and got sent off. Gordon Hughes said "Never mind, Ron." I replied "Gordon, if that had been a fight I'd have taken him in the second round." Well, someone must have heard us, because it went in the paper and suddenly I was "Cassius" McGarry.

'I decided that I needed a gimmick, something to get me in the public eye, so I had a chat with someone who was a printer and he said "What about this? Have Goals Will Travel." That's how it started.'

Between 1957–63 the actor Richard Boone played the part of Palladin, a knight-errant gunslinger, in the television series *Have Gun Will Travel.* This was the inspiration for Ron's gimmick.

'I said "Right, put Have goals will travel. Ron McGarry. Newcastle United." So he printed us about 15 cards and I started giving them out to some of the other team's players.'

The actual printed cards featured a picture of a footballer and the words 'Have goals will travel. R. McGARRY, (Newcastle United).'

'Before I knew it I was getting letters from the soldiers in Singapore, Hong Kong, Germany, saying "Send us a card". So I got more printed and even appeared on television with them. About three years ago I was at this New Year's Eve party and this woman came up to me and said "My dad died and he was a very good fan of yours. I'll give you this back". It was a

'Have goals will travel' card and I'd even signed it on the back. Even now, I get young lads asking me for them. It's surprising.

'I was in a club one night and a young lad was pointing over towards me. I thought "He's wanting something". Anyway, he came over and said "Mr McGarry, can I speak to you?" I said "Aye" and he replied "Do you remember me?" Well, I thought that there must've been something that I'd done for him, so I said "Oh yes, son". He said "I knew it. I sat on your knee when I was three. I told them you would know me". Off he went as happy as Larry. They never forget you.'

Ron had fond memories of the Toon Army from his playing days at St James' Park.

'When we were there, when we won the Second Division, the average gate was 44,000. It was a fantastic crowd for us. They were so fanatical. It used to be half a crown when we played. There were no season tickets, everybody queued. They used to stand there at one o'clock to get in. You need season tickets now because it's a big business.

'I remember going up the wing once and I heard Joe Harvey shouting "Pass, pass". This kid standing in the crowd said "Pass? He couldn't pass friggin' water". You could hear them. I remember in one game, someone got injured, and I'm sitting on the ball on the touchline. Well, I started keeping the ball up and I got the crowd to sing this song "McGarry's the best buy, the best buy". They were all singing it and Stan Anderson came up and said "You're a nutter". I said "I'm just entertaining the crowd". The next day there was a picture in the paper of me keeping the ball up. It was just a bit of fun.

'There were real characters in the game then. It's all different now. Players realised that they were just like a working man. That's all they were. They weren't really superstars. You were just somebody who had a better gift than someone working in a factory. That's all we were.'

Most players have recollections of certain special performances, as Ron explained.

'Northampton, when we beat them and we were both joint top of the table. We beat them 5–0 and I scored a hat-trick that day. That would be the best. But winning promotion in 1965 was good. We got promotion with six or seven games to go, which was a good achievement. They'd been waiting a long time to get back in the First Division at the time. It was a good team with quite a few characters.'

Ron was the top scorer with 16 goals in the 1964/65 promotion-winning season. He enjoyed a good relationship with manager Joe Harvey who first signed him for Workington Reds in 1960.

'I thought Joe Harvey was the best. I always remember one of his nights when we had to say something about him. I said "Joe, I can hear them on the terraces as I'm going through the middle saying 'Who picks that bastard?' What's a bastard,

Joe?" He said "Oh, it's a kid born out of wedlock". I said "But I was born in Whitehaven. They also keep saying that you're my father because I keep getting my place in the team."

'Joe Harvey was a manager and a half. He was like a psychiatrist really. He knew how to treat different players individually. I remember him saying to Trevor Hockey one day, when we were playing against Southampton, with big Martin Chivers their centre-forward, "When you get the chance, Trevor, give him a little kick on the ankle and get him riled". So, the match kicked off and Trevor ran straight from the wing and kicked him.

'Joe smoked a lot of cigarettes. He probably kept the companies going. He must have smoked 30 cigarettes sitting on the touchline watching a match. You were falling over the ash if you came near the dugout. He was a fantastic manager. He was like a father to me. I've walked down the steps "effing and blinding" at him, saying "Stick your club up your backside because I'm not coming back. I can play anywhere". Then the next day he didn't say anything. It was as if nothing had happened. If you said that sort of thing now, you would never play again.'

Goal scoring was Ron's job and when choosing a favourite, there were a few to select from.

'I scored quite a good one against Nottingham Forest from 30 yards. I hit it right in the far corner and got us the equaliser. I scored a few from long distances. There was none of this going into the penalty area like nowadays. As soon as I saw the whites of those goalposts I used to have a shot. Joe Harvey used to say "Hit it. One of them will go in".

'When I was playing for Workington Reds at Doncaster, I must have had 35 shots. They were going all over the place, but one went in. I scored the winner. It was 1–0. I watch games now and they always seem to want to be inside the box before they'll have a shot.'

Moving to Newcastle United was considered by Ron to be the highlight of his football career.

'I was playing at Bolton with a lot of internationals, but I couldn't settle there. When Joe came in, that was the best career move for me, signing for Newcastle. I was coming to a club with fanatical fans and if they liked you, it didn't matter what you did right or wrong, they loved you. As long as you were giving 100 percent, they were right behind you.

'You could walk out into the town and go into a pub, and they wouldn't let you buy a drink. Although you were getting more money than they were, they would still buy the pint to say they'd been in your company. They were fantastic supporters and that was my best career move.

'I was down at the ground the other week and I couldn't get in to see someone because it was a high profile area. I'd been in America the week before at Fort Knox. It was easier to get in there. They've got to take into consideration that if the fans don't come to watch them, they don't get paid. There's a hell of a lot of players getting good money who are just average players. They should appreciate the fans more.

'They should be sending different players to local schools to do a bit of coaching for them. We used to do all the talks and presentations for nothing. Then people started taking money. I've never taken a penny in my life.'

During Ron's time at Newcastle United, he came up against many tough defenders. I asked him about formidable opponents and also his heroes.

'Charlie Hurley was hard to play against. He was a good centre-half. At the time, there were a lot of good defenders around. If you played well against them, you were a good player. Most teams used to work on their defence in those days. If they had a good defence, they were usually successful.

'My first hero was Tommy Lawton. When I got into my teens, it was Stanley Matthews, Tom Finney, and Len Shackleton. When I got into football, it was Jackie Milburn. He was Mr Newcastle. I liked him, he was the greatest bloke you could ever meet. He would do anything for you. He was a smashing bloke. There were a lot of good players around then. They didn't have to be speed merchants because they could make the ball do the work.

'It's all changed now. They're not better players. They're faster but they're not better players. The game is so simple, but they seem to make it very hard for themselves.'

It is not surprising that there were many amusing events that occurred during Ron's era, given the characters around at the time. Here are a few to cherish.

'Well, we were playing Chester in the cup. I was standing on the line when Alan Suddick came up behind me and pulled down my shorts just as they were taking a free kick. I'm standing there with my shorts round my ankles while they're taking the free kick and Alan Suddick was just laughing his head off. I said "They could've scored". He said "You nearly did."'

In fact, Ron did score in the game, which Newcastle won 3–1 on 22 January 1966.

'I remember we had a promotion dinner one night at a nightclub and we had to buy our own beer. John McGrath said "Do you want a cigar?" I said "Aye, go on then. I don't smoke but I'll have a cigar for the night". He said "You'll have to buy your own". So I went up to the counter and said "You've got to give us a box of cigars on the club for the promotional dinner". I was given a box of cigars, so we started giving them around. John said "We'll get thrown out". We didn't.

'We were playing Middlesborough on Boxing Day and we beat them 2–0. Lord Westwood said to John McGrath and I "Come to the boardroom and have a drink". So, off we go to the boardroom and we're sitting having a drink with the chairman, Lord Westwood. Joe Harvey and the rest of the team are sitting on the bus waiting. As we got onto the bus with Lord Westwood, Joe was playing hell with us. I said "We've been with Lord Westwood". The chairman, Lord Westwood, said "You haven't been with me". Joe gave us a right rollicking, then he sent for us on the Monday and bollocked us again.

'I remember when Liam Tuohy told me about the time he was injured and went down to the treatment room. When he got there, Charlie Mitten, the manager, was there with two greyhounds under the lamps. He said to Liam "What do you want?" Liam said "I've been told to report for treatment". Charlie replied "Not today you haven't. These two are running tonight, you're not playing until Saturday. Come back tomorrow".

'We were playing away at Sheffield United and we were drawing 2–2. They won a corner, so I came back to defend it. When the ball came over, I don't know why but I caught it and gave away a penalty. We lost the game 3–2 and nobody spoke to me on the bus going home. To this day, I don't know why I did it.'

Ron's career at Newcastle United was to come to an unexpected and somewhat abrupt end.

'I remember I was at the Dolce Vita. I was at a dinner with the mayor in the afternoon and I got a phone call. The mayor said "Ron, Lord Westwood's on the phone for you". I said

"How does he know I'm in here?" Anyway, I go to the phone and Lord Westwood said "Ron, you're getting transferred to Barrow". I said "I'm not going to Barrow. I'm not going there". He replied "I'll tell you something, you go to Barrow or you don't play football again". That was it, I had to go to Barrow. So, when I was leaving, I said "I've always wanted to be a barrow boy."'

Ron McGarry left Newcastle United in March 1967, having been transferred to Barrow for £3,500. There was little doubt that during his five years at St James' Park he gave his all on the pitch and proved that, long before the Keegan years, footballers could also be entertainers. Ron's great sense of humour did not desert him when he left Newcastle.

In 1968, Ron was the player-coach with Bolgownie, Australia.

'I remember when I was in Australia and the Prime Minister sent for me. He said "Ron, there's not enough room in this country for two celebrities". About six weeks later he was killed in a shark attack.'

Ron McGarry would never consider himself to have been a footballing superstar, but with his commitment to the game and to the supporters, there was little doubt that he was certainly a star.

GORDON MARSHALL
(1963–68)

GORDON Marshall was born in Farnham, Surrey on 2 July 1939, but was brought up in Edinburgh, Scotland. He signed for Newcastle United from Heart of Midlothian in June 1963 for £18,500. It has often been said that goalkeepers are in reality frustrated centre-forwards. Gordon admits that he was no exception.

'I played them all at school, football, cricket, basketball, everything. I think what happens is, there's something that you get along better at and have more success at. That's what happened with the football. I finished up getting more success with it, with the goalkeeping. You just start concentrating more on that.

'You get mates and you play as a juvenile. On a Saturday, you'd play in the morning and the afternoon. Throughout the summer nights, you're playing three times a week. Everybody was the same. I don't think that there were many other sports you could play. Football was what everybody wanted. Well, at the schools I went to, anyway.

'To tell you the truth, I was a big stiffy. I wanted to be a centre-forward, scoring a lot of goals, something like that. You go along for the school trials and things like that, and it finished up, all my mates got picked and I didn't get picked. And they'd say "Right, we've one position left, the goalkeeper. Have we got a goalkeeper?" You'd say "Aye, yes, me", just to get in the team. So that's how it all started. I used to like to play out of goal. Even when I played professionally, you had all these five-a-side knockabout games and I liked playing out as well, same as anybody.'

Gordon soon discovered that he was putting his dreams of becoming a centre-forward to one side as he started to take more notice of the men between the posts.

'As a kid brought up in Edinburgh, my local team was Hearts. My dad and all my uncles used to go to Tynecastle and they used to stand at the same spot every week at the back of the goal. I used to go along. Sometimes you were interested in the game and other times you were running around playing tig. You were at that age.

'When I first started playing in goal, there was a lad,

Jimmy Brown, who played in goal for Hearts, and I was mesmerised. I just used to go and watch him. He was such a colourful character and he was always immaculate. He was spotless. He walked about the goalmouth, touching each post. He never stood still. These were the little things you used to watch.

'Then I found myself watching other goalkeepers. Another lad at Queen of the South, Roy Henderson, used to sit on the wall and chat with the crowd. There were characters in the game in those days who were local lads that you took a shine to. Then I started reading about a wider sphere of goalkeepers.

'When I finished up signing for Hearts, my first club, we did a tour of America and we had to go over by boat. How it worked, we had an English team and a Scottish team and we met four times throughout America. It was a sort of test match series, promoting the game over there. The other team was Manchester City and their goalkeeper was the famous Bert Trautmann, the ex-prisoner of war. That was a couple of years after he had broken his neck. Chatting with him was unbelievable. I was only 17 at the time.'

It was a landmark legal battle that ultimately influenced Gordon's decision to move south of the border. Newcastle United player George Eastham took the club to court over the maximum wage that was in force at the time.

'I'd actually been with Hearts for seven years and at that time, when I was playing in Scotland, there was the maximum on. When the maximum came off with the George Eastham case, that started everything rolling.

'Johnny Haynes became the first £100 a week player. Then the lid came right off in Scotland. All the good players started to drift down south. Dave Mackay went to Tottenham, Alec

87

Young went to Everton. George Thompson also went to Everton. I felt the same that this was where to go.

'I remember, I was playing with Hearts in an Inter Cities Fairs Cup game away against Inter Milan. Coming back in the plane, I'm thinking to myself that this game is bigger than just Scotland. I actually asked to be allowed to leave at the time and was refused. That was the year that I was getting married.

'The week before I was actually due to get married, I got a phone call on the Friday night from Hearts. It was Tommy Walker, the manager, and he wanted me to go in on the Monday morning. Stan Seymour and Joe Harvey were coming up from Newcastle, wanting to have a chat. They'd agreed a price for me. That was the Friday, so I had all weekend to think about it.

'I just couldn't believe it. This was the weekend before I was due to get married. We'd bought a house and everything. I never even told my wife-to-be. I just went in on the Monday morning and within half-an-hour I was signing for Newcastle United. I then had to go home and tell my wife-to-be that we were moving. At the time I thought that was what I wanted and that's probably why it took me a good year to settle at Newcastle.'

They, whoever they happen to be, often say that first impressions are important. Gordon was very much aware of this after moving to his new club.

'When I first went down to Newcastle, they must have thought, what's this that we've signed. Joe must have said "Oh dear me", or words to that effect. I was terrible. I think that getting married and moving house, away from home, everything happened so much and so quick. But we look back today and I still feel it's the best move I ever made.'

Gordon thought that he had moved to a 'big' club in England, but sometimes first impressions can also be deceptive.

'I put English football way up there and it's supposed to be the cream. But the funny thing was that when I got there, they weren't as big time a club as what Hearts were. When I say big time, it was typical, I got a goalkeeper's jersey handed to me and it was one of these moth-eaten things where the sleeves creep up. With me being six foot two, it couldn't even go inside my pants.

'I remember a reporter once saying to me "Why do you wear your jersey outside your pants?" I said "Because it won't stay inside. Every time I bend down, it comes out". I couldn't say anything about it because the club was supplied by Stan Seymour in town at the time. In those days, we didn't have gloves either. I wanted to go back to Hearts to get a yellow jersey, but I wasn't allowed to. English goalkeepers weren't allowed to wear yellow. I don't know why that was the case. So, I finished up wearing a blue one and a green one.'

I asked Gordon to recollect his memories of St James' Park on matchdays.

'In those days, you never really thought about the stadium. You had to be in the ground well over an hour before kick-off. We used to average 34,000 at home. Newcastle United was one of the first clubs to have each turnstile keep a running total. We were on crowd bonus at the time. There was a small room where someone could see the total clicking up on each turnstile and there was a running total of what the gate was.

"I remember that people used to hang around outside and that. There was none of this warming up like they do nowadays. My warm up was to get the ball in the shower room and throw it against the wall. We just kept warm in the dressing room. I never used to like to get my pants dirty before the game.

'When I parked my car at the ground, I could walk past my wife, my best friend, or anyone who knew me, on my way inside. I wouldn't see them. It must have looked ignorant. I was so focused. Really, what you wanted to do was to get into the dressing room and shut everything else off. You didn't want to be bothered with tickets or anything else.

'It was get in the dressing room and get the banter going between the players. We prepared that way. I used to have the two or three hours before the game getting prepared. It was great once you got into the dressing room, you'd got something to do.'

I asked Gordon about his superstitions on matchdays.

'You had little superstitions. You wore the same suit or you wore the same tie. You put your pants on last. There was always something. It was funny, you could look around the dressing room and some people would go really quiet and other people couldn't stop talking. Other people would be thinking about their horse that had run. Everybody had their own way of preparing themselves.

'Joe Harvey was good on man-management. He never used to say all that much, but he had Ron McGarry in the dressing room and he was just a joke a minute. Latterly, when the chips were down and we were going for promotion, Ron wasn't playing, but he was in that dressing room all the time. He broke the tension with his continual chatting and joking. It was a happy dressing room.

'I remember Liverpool coming to play and I went into their dressing room for autographs. And who's in there? Jimmy Tarbuck. He used to travel everywhere. What a dressing room that must have been as well. That was the best sort of release before the game. But, getting back to superstitions, you'd do them and you'd have a not so clever game, so you'd change them. You'd maybe wear the same tie for three or four weeks and then after a bad game you'd think that it was a waste of time.'

After moving to Newcastle United, Gordon found that the progress being made in football didn't actually help him personally.

'I actually found that the game started changing a hell of a lot. Goalkeeping started changing. When I first played, we didn't wear gloves. You caught the ball and you bounced it, using your full penalty area. Then the Continental goalkeeper came in and started time wasting. I remember when it started that you could only take four steps. I started getting myself in a hell of a mess.

'I could only kick the ball with my left peg. We only had four steps, so if you made a move on that side and the opposing player was standing on that side, you couldn't clear it properly. It would have been good if we'd had goalkeeping coaches when I was playing. This back pass rule, I don't know if I would have been able to cope with it. You can get the ball passed back from the right-back, so you've got to kick it down the right side. You have got to be two-footed today.

'I must admit that at the time I started feeling the pressure with all the different rules coming in. I couldn't cope with it all at the time and I'm sure that's why my form started to dip. I started to struggle a bit. It was all to do with the new rules.'

Gordon was asked to recall what he considered to be his best personal performance in goal for Newcastle United.

'I think that one of my best performances was against Liverpool at the Park one day.'

Perhaps I should explain that Gordon referred to St James' Park simply as 'the Park' during our conversation.

'It was at the time when I wasn't a regular in the team and the crowd was giving me a bit of stick as well. It was maybe time for me to move on, that sort of thing. That particular game, I had a good game. We were playing against Ian St John, big Ron Yeats, and a Liverpool team that was really flying. I think that would have been my best game at the Park, being at home with Newcastle against Liverpool.

'The other game that comes to mind would have been when we were in the old Second Division. We played at Southampton and we had to get a result there. We were well ahead in the season and then we started to slip up. We started to have a bit of a rocky time. Other clubs were catching up with us. Then we went to Southampton and it was one of my best games as well. They were flying at the time as well.'

As a goalkeeper, you are the last line of defence, albeit in a solo position. I asked Gordon if he could recall any particular opponents who stood out for him.

'Not really, you had to be aware of everybody. A big centre-forward, height-wise, was not a problem. You usually found that a nice high ball would come in and that was never a worry to me. You could read the high ball. I would say that it was the likes of Jimmy Greaves, George Best, and other players whose skill on the ball was unpredictable. You never knew what they were going to do with it.'

Gordon had fond memories of the Newcastle United supporters and never forgot the impact that they could make on a game.

'They were brilliant, just brilliant. Mind, they could be really quiet for a bit, but when they really got going, they got behind you. The sort of lift that you used to get, I used to think I can't afford to make a mistake here, I mustn't make a mistake. You were carried away with them. It's a tremendous feeling when they're really going with you. It's like an extra man. It's a brilliant adrenaline rush that it gives you.

'The noise that they used to make was great. They used to turn up and watch the grass grow. I remember I had a conversation with Dave Hilley one day and he said "They'd turn up and watch the grass grow. They're not real. Imagine if we could play better. Imagine if we were a really good team, what it would be like".

'Newcastle is a big club, as big as any club. They are nowadays, but when you go back to the 1960s, it was tremendous. When I left and went back to Scotland, you had to be there 45 minutes before the game started. I'd be driving up to the ground thinking I'd made a mistake and we were playing away. The crowds were so small. It was much harder. Playing at Newcastle, you'd get so pumped up and focused.'

When you are the last line of defence, it is perhaps more obvious to the watching public when you make a mistake. It is something that you dread and it is even worse when the television cameras are present to beam your blunder across the whole country. Of course nowadays, there are numerous videos of football blunders on sale. In this respect, Gordon is probably delighted to have been ahead of his time.

'When I was saying about the crowds getting going and you not wanting to make a mistake, I was playing against Manchester United at the Park and we were beating them 2–1. We were playing them off the park. The crowd was baying for the final whistle.

'Brennan was going down the line and he hits this cross. It was a goalkeeper's ball and I thought, what a dolly this is. I actually moved and went underneath it. He hadn't actually kicked it, he'd sliced it. Well, it drifted and drifted right overhead, hit the far post, and went in the back of the net. We got the ball out of the net, centred it, and then the final whistle went. It was 2–2.

'Oh, I was gutted and it was shown on *Match of the Day*. When you've done that, I was sick. I was actually frightened to go out that night. With it being on television, they played it that night, they played it on the Sunday, they played it midweek, and then they played it the following week. I just couldn't get away from it. I'd made that mistake and I felt awful.

'I remember the following week, we were at Coventry. I'm standing in the toilet when we were in the hotel, pre-match, and this bloke walks in. He's standing next to me in the toilet and he says "Are you going to the game today?" I said "Aye". He obviously didn't know who I was. He said "I hope to hell they're not playing that bugger Marshall. Did you see that goal he let in last week?" I said "I know, what a goal. What a dumpling. Who'd be a goalie?"'

As mentioned earlier, Gordon felt that his form was being affected by the changing rules in the game that were specifically shaping the way goalkeepers had to play. He was also affected by the emerging squad rotation, an accepted feature of the modern game. It is not that popular with players today and it was no different when Gordon was at Newcastle.

'The squad system was starting to come in, but it was never something that anybody liked. Everybody wanted to play.'

It was the squad system and his emerging struggle with the changing rules in football that ultimately led to Gordon moving on. He first transferred to Nottingham Forest in 1968, but soon discovered that he had made a mistake. He eventually returned to Scotland to continue his career and was much more settled.

Looking back, Gordon would no doubt have benefited greatly from the expertise of the modern-day goalkeeping coaches. He certainly didn't lack the strength or commitment required of a goalkeeper, but he would perhaps have had the opportunity to have been coached to use both feet. During his football career Gordon was a respected professional and I suppose even the most gifted player can be forgiven for being a dumpling on one occasion.

Chapter 8

WYN DAVIES
(1966–71)

RONALD Wyn Davies was born in Caernarfon, north Wales, on 20 March 1942. He signed for Newcastle United from Bolton Wanderers in October 1966 for £80,000. Wyn made 216 senior starts for Newcastle and scored 53 goals. He won 34 full international caps playing for Wales. Wyn was a cult hero on Tyneside, playing as centre-forward, with his performances helping to spearhead Newcastle United's success in Europe in the Inter Cities Fairs cup in 1969. Like so many professional footballers, Wyn's love for the game developed at an early age.

'It was at school really. It first started at school. I just loved playing football, even then, especially after school in the street. In those days, we used to put out coats as goalposts. It's funny, I don't know how old I was, but I remember one day we had this old football, a leather one. I remember this chap watching us playing football and we used to play until it was dark. There was a lamp where we used to play and this chap painted our ball white. He put white gloss on it, so that we could see it in the dark. I'm talking about the old ball and it was rock hard in those days. I loved anything to do with sport, even at school. At football, I was only a junior, but I was playing for the seniors at school. So, it went on from there.'

Wyn's early football hero was, not surprisingly, a fellow Welshman.

'As a child I vaguely remember watching only one player, he was always my hero, the late John Charles, the 'Gentle Giant'. Looking back then, I remember Stanley Matthews, but only from the Cup Finals that I used to see. The first Cup Final I ever saw, on my brother's mate's black and white telly, was Newcastle United playing against Manchester City in 1955. It's funny, at my age at that time, you wonder what you're going to do when you leave school. Not realising it at the time, I was sitting there watching two clubs that I would actually end up playing for, not knowing I would go on to become a professional footballer.

'So, it all started then, and when I left school I went into the quarries. It was through my uncle one day asking me if I'd like a game of football. I was over the moon. My first game was at Bangor and I didn't play well at all. I had the opportunity to play a second time and I actually played very well. I played for

Llanberis and then I signed for Caernarfon, my home town. I used to get 10 bob. I was only a young kid really. I remember the manager getting me a pair of spikes to make me run quicker.'

When Wyn became a professional footballer, little did he realise that he would have some big names to follow.

'When I went to Bolton, I had to fill the boots of the centre-forward, the legend Nat Lofthouse. It's funny and strange, when I went to Newcastle, it was the same there, the legend Jackie Milburn. I thought I did reasonably well at Bolton and at Newcastle. To fill the boots of those legends, it was quite hard.'

Wyn's expected transfer to Newcastle United did not go through at the first attempt. At the time, he appeared to have been given some advice that was not welcomed by the Newcastle directors.

'Well, the first time, it didn't come off. At the time, it was Lord Westwood who was chairman and they came down to Bolton to see me. There were one or two well-known players giving me advice because I had no agent then. I was told, just tell them that you've got 24 hours to think about it. It was important to me because I was going a long way away from home. I was told by these players to tell them that I wanted £70 a week and £7,000 in my hand, and 24 hours to make up my mind.

'I remember that all these directors from Newcastle came down that day. I was in the boardroom and I was sitting there as if I was the boss. Well, I was playing for Wales the following week, but they wanted me to play on the Saturday against Spurs at home. What happened, the deal didn't go through. I was told afterwards that they'd seen me playing on Good Friday at Newcastle, when they were promoted with Northampton, and big John McGrath was marking me. I must admit, I had a great afternoon. I hit the bar a few times with headers, so the supporters and perhaps Joe Harvey must have seen something a bit special at the time. Apparently, John put me out of the game.

'The following Monday, Newcastle were playing at Bolton, but I couldn't play. A few months later, Newcastle came back in for me and this time I signed for them. I must admit that it was the best move I've ever made, because it was fantastic up there. Of course, the first game, we were beaten by Sunderland and I thought, what a start for me. Anyway, I thought that Albert Bennett and I did quite well at the time.'

I asked Wyn to recall his memories of matchdays at St James' Park.

'At the time, I was in digs in Heaton, so it was just a question of getting up, having a light meal, and just sort of make my way up to the ground. There was nothing special, I was a bit nervous. In the end, I had Tommy Gibb in digs with me and eventually I got Jimmy Smith as well, when we moved to Pelton, out of town. I know that I used to elastoplast my feet, then put my socks on, then put my boots on and then, believe it or not, I used to put my feet in water just to soften the boots up.'

Newcastle United's success in the Inter Cities Fairs Cup in 1969 was a great adventure for Wyn personally.

'As a kid, watching Newcastle play Manchester City on the television, I was thinking to myself how great it would be to get to Wembley. Newcastle were always good to watch in the cup.

'I've always said, I like a bet and I think that Newcastle were 33–1 to win the Fairs Cup, but I never bothered to put any money on them. We played Feyenoord at home and we beat them 4–0. Then we went over there and I had a bad injury. We got beat, but we won on the aggregate. I remember going up to St James' Park after the matches, upstairs with some of the directors and their wives, and I stupidly said to them "I'll tell

you what I'll do. If we win this competition, I'll shave my hair off". All of a sudden, we were getting near, with only two or three games to go. People were asking me if I was really going to do it and I said "Don't remind me".

'There were hard games, but it was a good team spirit. I surprised myself really. When we played the first leg of the final at St James' Park, Bobby Moncur got two goals and we always said in training that Bobby would stay on the opposing goal-line and I'd be outside the box trying to head the ball towards the goal. If the ball got to him, he could swivel and try to get it in. Well, I remember on that night, he had scored two goals and he was on the goal-line. Pop Robson got a corner ball over and I'm really belting on to this ball from outside the box. All of a sudden, I didn't realise it but Bobby, probably thinking that he was going for a hat-trick, was backing out. That was the moment that I smashed my cheekbone against the back of Bobby's head.

'I remember coming in at the end of the game and the first thing that I did, with all my gear still on, was to go into the cold shower. Then I remember Bobby coming in and he said "Wyn, are you alright?" Well, I just said "Bobby, for **** sake, **** off will you". I was really mad because it had come right up and I was thinking, when's the second leg? They were going to operate on the following day, which meant that I wouldn't have been able to play in the final. I just said "I'm not having that. I want to play in the final". So, that was it, the operation was put off until after the second leg of the final.

'When we won the Cup, it was brilliant. Coming back to Newcastle to see all the fans, from the airport all the way down to the ground, it was unbelievable. At the ground, I was told that I was only allowed to have one drink and that really annoyed me, because all the lads were really going to town. I had to go to the hospital round the back of the ground at teatime that day. I got the cheekbone done and fair enough, three months afterwards, they had a party for me.

'The Newcastle supporters were fanatical. They were brilliant, but they could turn. My mate Tommy Gibb, many a time Joe Harvey would say "You're not really giving the lad a chance here, so I might have to just play him away from home". What Tommy did one day, he gave the old two fingers at them. Some of them must have had a go at him. They never forgave him for that for a long time, but they did eventually when we came to the Fairs Cup because everybody played well.'

Wyn's battling style of play frequently led to very physical confrontations with opposing defenders. Playing through the pain barrier with injuries was not all that unusual for him.

'The thing is, in those days, we didn't have a rotational squad. I never did believe in it, but we were given cortisones. All the players who had cortisones had problems afterwards.

'In the Fairs Cup competition, I was playing over in Feyenoord and I had a bang on my shin. It came up like a balloon afterwards, but I put a cold compress on it. I remember coming back to Newcastle, I went to the treatment room, and Alex Mutch had done my bandage. From my knee down to my foot, it was black. I had a haematoma. Anyway, it went down and I remember saying to Joe that there was something not right. My foot was burning. I had this burning sensation in my foot. What had happened was, the blood wasn't circulating and it was blocked.

'I went to a hospital in Jesmond and I had to have my foot in the air for a whole week. Monday to Friday it was yellow. Believe it or not, I was playing the following day, the Saturday, against Leeds, after being a whole week with my foot up in the air. It was funny, I scored and it was 2–1 to us. I just knew that there had been something wrong.

'I finished up having another operation at the same hospital, it was for bloody piles. Believe it or not, I was hooked up with my legs apart and I remember Bob Rutherford, the doctor, coming into the operating room with a bloody great cigar in his mouth. You would've thought that he was a butcher running a butcher's shop. I've had a few bangs in my time and they're catching up with me now unfortunately.'

Wyn's choice of best performance was a particular cup game.

'It was an FA Cup game and I scored a hat-trick, but I wasn't allowed to keep the ball. I must admit that they were three cracking goals that I scored. It was at Coventry. They were in the First Division then and they had some good players. That day, I couldn't believe my eyes, I hit one from 25 yards and it flew past the keeper. The last one was a header on a right angle. That game stands out because I think that was the only hat-trick I had scored for Newcastle.'

Wyn chose to highlight two special goals, one scored for Bolton Wanderers and the other for Newcastle United, as his personal favourites.

'The best goal I ever scored in my career, believe it or not, I never saw it. It was at Sheffield Wednesday and Peter Swan was centre-half. I remember I was in my own half, just coming up to the centre spot, and I went about 10 yards into their half. All I remember was Peter Swan coming up and someone shouting 'Shoot, shoot!' Well, it was the same as in golf, you keep your head down, and I took two yards run-up with the ball and I hit it. All of a sudden, as I lifted my head up, the 'keeper's got the ball in his hands. All the Bolton players were coming up to me and shaking my hand. I said "What's happened?" and they said "You've bloody scored". It must have hit the stanchion inside at the time, bounced back out, and the 'keeper must have caught it in his hands. That must have been about 40 yards, I'm not kidding you, and I never saw it. It was never on television, so I've never seen it to this day.

'At Newcastle, for excitement, there was a minute to go, it was against Arsenal 1–1 at St James', and I remember Bob Wilson was in goal. When Pop Robson took the corner kick, with him being a right-footer, the ball went out and then came back towards the goal. Bob Wilson definitely thought it was going out for a goal-kick, because it had a right bend on it, but it came to me in a crowded goalmouth. I went up and I headed it in the top corner. That must have excited me because every time I scored at Newcastle, I always looked as though I was disappointed. The only goal where my hands were in the air was the Arsenal one. There were only seconds to go and we finished up winning it 2–1.'

As a centre-forward Wyn played against some great defenders.

'The one I never did like playing against was Bob McKinlay. He played centre-half for Nottingham Forest. It was great fun playing against Ron Yeates and Brian Labone of Everton. There was another centre-half who was five-foot nowt, that was Joe Shaw of Sheffield United. He could read the game brilliantly. I'd always gone for flicks for the inside-forward to go past me. I remember I could hear Joe breathing behind me and I thought, I'll get him here. When the ball came to me and I flicked it on, he'd gone 10 to 12 yards behind me, and he chested the ball down and played it.'

During his playing career with Newcastle United, Wyn achieved cult status with the supporters and he is still held in high esteem after all the years since he left the club. This is something that never ceases to amaze him.

'They were brilliant. They were the tops, really. It was funny, two seasons ago, I was invited to the Newcastle-Bolton match at St James' Park. I went on the pitch at half-time and it came over the loudspeaker "Please welcome the ex-Newcastle United and Bolton Wanderers star, Wyn Davies". As I'm walking over to the middle, all of a sudden they were singing "You'll not see nothing like the Mighty Wyn". There's me thinking to myself, how do they know that song? I left in 1971 and there I was, all these years later. There would probably have been a few old fellas there that day, but I was absolutely amazed. The supporters had given me the "Mighty Wyn" and the "Wyn the leap" sort of thing.

'I've got some old photos and people often say to me "You are high there, aren't you?" You don't realise, because you're tall you expect to get up high. People used to say "But how do you hang there?" At the time, I didn't realise that I was hanging in the air. I was tall and should've been able to jump and I suppose able to hang in the air.'

Wyn recalled one particular incident when he gave some of the lads a bit of an unwelcome surprise.

'I wasn't really embarrassed, but the lads were at the time. We had a sauna at Newcastle and it was bloody great. It was brilliant and all that. We used to add this water on it. Well, one day, there was John McGrath, Jim Iley, Albert Bennett, Pop, Clarkie, and everyone was in there. What I did that day, I peed didn't I. But, I didn't pee on it, I had it in a little glass and I put it on where you usually put the spoonful of water, you see. Within a couple of seconds, they all went "Bloody hell!" If it had been on a main street with women going past, they would've seen them all running out of that sauna. But that was just a bit of fun, really. Well, I thought it was at the time, anyway.'

Wyn Davies gave Newcastle United supporters five years of exciting football. His bravery, especially in the European adventures, added to his status on Tyneside and to the Toon Army, he always will be the 'Mighty Wyn'. Looking back to Wyn's childhood, the man who painted the football white may not have recognised the true potential of one of the boys playing in the street. However, his paintbrush illuminated the ball for one young lad in particular, who later illuminated St James' Park with his own glossy performances.

Chapter 9

KEITH DYSON

(1967–71)

KEITH Dyson was born in Blackhill, County Durham, on 10 February 1950. He signed as an apprentice with Newcastle United in 1967 and signed professional in August 1968. As a talented young striker, Keith made 92 senior starts for Newcastle United and scored 26 goals. Keith seemed destined to be a footballer from a very early age.

'Right from the age of about four, well actually from the day that I was born really, outside our house was a field which belonged to the local council, but it was used by the local schools and as a play area by us. So, as soon as I had a spare moment, I was straight out of the garden into the field to join in the kickabout games. So I was playing every night from the age of four years right up to when I signed professional. It was just a natural activity for me to do.

'In the days when I went to Newcastle United, you signed on as an associate schoolboy and went down on Tuesday and Thursday nights, then you went through the juniors and the reserves. I actually signed professional at 18.'

I asked Keith for his recollections of the training regime at Newcastle in the late 1960s.

'Generally, training was pretty good. You had a couple of the old-school type people there, like Joe Richardson, running the reserves. Being the old-school type, he would send you out for 10 laps running round the cinder track just to warm you up. Then you would get into one penalty box and you would have to sprint to the other penalty box. It was always that kind of tradition, a few laps, a few long sprints, a few shorter sprints, and then it was off you go. There were no tactics or anything like that.

'Some of the memories would be, getting changed, getting your kit on, running up to Hunters Moor, getting involved in reserves or first-team squads. If you were asked to be in the first-team squad, it was a big thing among all the people. That was always a pointer towards what the manager was thinking about for the Saturday team selection. Then it just went on from there. We used to have training sessions down on the beach, if they thought that it was a good idea at the time. We used to have five-a-side games on the beach. They were quite aggressive. Then, we also had golf days.'

Keith found himself playing in Newcastle United's first team very soon after signing professional. He wasn't quite prepared for the transition. He recalled a typical Saturday when Newcastle were playing at home at St James' Park.

'A home game, there was nothing special. It was get comfortable at home, have breakfast, then maybe something light, a slice of toast at around 12 o'clock. When I started off, I was in the first team very quickly, within six weeks of signing professional, and I had a big problem with not having a car. I used to go down to the town by bus, the number 11 bus from Consett, and I was getting on the bus with the fans after 12 o'clock. I found that a little bit unsettling because you couldn't sort of relax and chill out, or get that bit focused. You were getting "Oh, there's Keith Dyson" or whatever, and it was like that going back after the match as well. I would be on the bus for about 40 minutes and you would get all the fans travelling with you. It wasn't a private occasion. I didn't really like that.

'So I was determined that one of the first things to do was to get a car. I didn't actually get my own car until something like February 1970. I had signed professional in August 1968, so it took a while. For the match itself, it was a case of get down on the bus, get into the dressing room, make sure your kit was all there, your boots were there, and walk on the pitch. That was definitely true of away games, walking on the pitch. Then you'd go back inside, start getting changed about twenty past two, and just fill in the time, doing a few stretches. You couldn't warm up as they do now. Then we probably had a bit of a team talk, a bit of a 'let's get cracking' talk about twenty to three, probably by Joe Harvey or Jim Smith. We actually moved on more to tactics in my later stages.'

Keith supported Newcastle United as a child and later went

on to play for his home team. He recalled the atmosphere on matchdays.

'The packed sardines picture just floods back. I mean, there were so many people there and the atmosphere was fantastic, but you were packed in. But, it was fantastic, the chanting and the noise was brilliant. There's the same noise now, but it has a different feel to it. It still has its own special atmosphere now, but back then it was just open sides. The Leazes End was the big thing. If you could do well at the Leazes End and get them chanting your name or score a goal at that end, it was great.

'I always remember the bevel on the pitch at St James' Park, but I think that's gone now. When you were in the dugout watching a match, I doubt that Joe Harvey could see the ball on the other side of the pitch. There was that much of a bevel on it. When I used to watch the team from the age of nine with neighbours, we used to sit on the Popular side with that little wall. It was just tremendous, it was great.

'Newcastle United, that was the team I was going for all the time. When you live at Consett, it's either Sunderland or Newcastle, but predominantly Newcastle. Sunderland was awkward to get to, so Newcastle was always my team. But I was always proud of being from County Durham. As a schoolboy, there was always a big rivalry between County Durham and Northumberland.'

Keith had to make another significant transition, from being a football supporter to playing for the team that he had supported. He recalled how the team would lift the crowd and equally how the crowd would lift the team. In later life, Keith was to return to the scene of his playing days and he found the experience of being in the crowd once again to be rather different from what he had remembered from his childhood and his time spent on the pitch at St James' Park.

'The supporters will give you a certain patience that they will let run for maybe 30 to 40 minutes, but if it's not happening, they will start to get a bit anxious and start criticising. You've just got to hope for a good start and when things are going well, then the atmosphere is also good. It is difficult to say who is the leader of it all. I went to see the Newcastle-Manchester United game at the start of the season and I was at the Gallowgate End. I was absolutely amazed at the vitriol shouted against some of the players and the manager when things didn't seem to be going well. I thought that one guy was going to have a heart attack actually. It was quite an eye-opener. They really don't hold back when they start criticising. But, generally they are a great set of people.'

In more recent times, Newcastle United supporters have enjoyed the thrills and spills of European football, watching the team play in the UEFA Cup and the Champions League. During Keith's time at St James' Park, Newcastle United played in the Inter Cities Fairs Cup, the forerunner to the UEFA Cup, for three consecutive seasons. Newcastle United qualified for the Fairs Cup in 1968/69 by virtue of the old 'one team per city' rule, having finished a mere 10th in the league the previous season. To Keith and the rest of the Newcastle United squad, that was the rule and they were determined to enjoy the experience.

When recalling memorable performances, it was not surprising that Keith chose one of the local derby games and one from Newcastle United's European adventures.

'Newcastle versus Sunderland 1969. It was on television. We beat them 3–0. I scored twice and Wyn Davies scored the other one. I just remember the first goal, a kick from our keeper Willie McFaul going towards the Leazes End, and Wyn Davies flicked it on. I just followed through. I was on the right-hand corner of the penalty box, probably about four yards away, not even in the box, and I just let fly. I thought that I'd have a go at it and it skimmed off the centre-half's head and it went in the far top corner. The 'keeper had no chance. Then it just got better and better. We comprehensively beat them 3–0. So, that was a great memory because 56,000 people were there to see it.

'The most memorable European performance for me was against Anderlecht. To me, it was part of three years of Fairs Cup football, 1968–70. I didn't get completely involved in the 1968/69 one when they won the trophy, but the next season was more important to me personally. That next season, we were heading for the semi-final and we played in the quarter-final against Anderlecht. Of course, we were 2–0 down from the away leg, coming back to Newcastle. Pop Robson was in fantastic form for a couple of years really and he struck a twenty-five yarder and got us back to 2–2. Then I think that there was about three minutes to go when Bobby Moncur took this free-kick from near the dugout area towards the Leazes End. I just got on the end of it and made it 3–2 on aggregate.

'So we were actually winning then, but from the kick-off they played the ball forward and it rebounded to Thomas Nordahl who took two strides and from well outside the box, let fly and of course he scored. They had got the equaliser with a minute to go and that meant that they went through on the away goals rule. That was a killer for me and for many other people, because it changed everything. We would have been in the semi-final again, with a chance of winning the Fairs Cup again. The crowds were as high as ever and we would have played against Arsenal in the semi-final.'

During his time playing for Newcastle United, Keith scored 26 goals for the first team. I asked him if he had a favourite goal.

'There were a few actually. I tended to go for a lot of shots. Another one that sticks in my mind was against Nottingham Forest at home. Again, kicking towards the Leazes End, for some reason one of their players started dribbling the ball out near the byline of the goal, just outside the box. I just harassed him and won the ball back. I then cut inside a little bit, about six yards from the line, and again I just let fly. I remember Wyn Davies shouting for a pass across. Anyway, I let fly and it nestled in the top corner in the stanchion. It was just a tremendous feeling because I could imagine Joe Harvey in the dugout thinking what a ridiculous shot to make.'

Since Keith played professional football with Newcastle, the game has changed in so many ways, both on and off the field. So many goals are scored from close range nowadays, which makes the spectacular volley from long distance all that more spectacular.

'That's a key difference nowadays, the lack of shots. Players just don't get to the byline anymore to get crosses over. We had such good players at Newcastle in my time, yet I suppose we also had such poor games at times in the league, it was unbelievable.'

Throughout Keith's time at Newcastle United, Joe Harvey was manager.

'Joe signed me in person, along with Benny Craig, who was the reserves team coach. He was tough and uncompromising. You see, then you didn't get any arms around your shoulders type of behaviour, it was all manly. You wouldn't get anybody coming up saying "We're resting you because you've had a hard time there. You're young, give yourself a few games, you did really well, but have a look at your left foot or right foot". You were either in or you were out. There was no explanation and you just got on with it.

Nowadays it wouldn't happen like that. You'd get constantly coached.'

At the start of Keith's professional career, he was a young striker, a mere 18 years of age, and he came face to face with some big, tough defenders. When I asked Keith about formidable opponents, there were quite a few of them, mostly from one team.

'Every team that we played against was full of characters, but it has got to be Leeds United. There was Norman Hunter, Jack Charlton, and Billy Bremner. In fact, that whole team was tough to play against. They were just hard, if you understand what I'm saying. They had a reputation for being hard.'

Before playing for Newcastle United, Keith used to go and watch them play as a youngster. He recalled some of his heroes.

'I used to watch people like Len White. I probably just caught the end of his time there. Then, I often say to people, I saw the best half-back line arguably in Newcastle's colours. There was Stan Anderson, John McGrath, and Jim Iley. I thought that they were fantastic. They just knocked the ball about like you wouldn't believe it, even when you saw it. Jim Iley would hit a ball from left-half to the right-wing. Alan Suddick was also a great player.

'Lots of people were just fazed by watching Wyn Davies when he first came to Newcastle. How he would power up into the air and he would hit balls against the bar and all that. Sometimes that would be more exciting than when he actually scored a goal. It was a real honour playing alongside Wyn, dovetailing and trying to get on the end of his flick-ons. I started off playing in such an exciting time. Wyn Davies was a big plus to me.'

I asked Keith if he thought that he would have fitted into the current Newcastle United team had he been born in the mid-1980s.

'Some people would say that I lacked pace, but I worked hard on that. Malcolm Macdonald and Alan Shearer would have been a better combination. I was more of a shielder kind of player, pushing people in for chances, shield the ball, pass it on, make chances. Alan Shearer would have been great to play alongside, but I don't know if it would have worked.

'Jimmy Smith was something else. He would have loved playing today and the supporters would have loved watching him play. I always remember making runs and Jimmy would spot me. He saw moves ahead of other people. It was just a natural talent to him. He was one of the greatest passers of the ball.'

Keith had fond memories of the away trips with Newcastle United, particularly in Europe and especially with him still being a young lad.

'There were lots of memories, daft things that you probably wouldn't see nowadays. You'd get Wyn Davies, down at Spurs before the match, he'd be opening the window of the dressing room, making contact with some of his relatives or whoever it was, talking in Welsh and giving them tickets through the window.

'All of the Fairs Cup trips were fantastic. Going abroad, it was just so exciting. Going to France, Holland, Belgium and Portugal, it was just non-stop and it was full of great and funny memories. We'd be playing cards, cracking jokes, just enjoying ourselves because they were like four-day trips in the Fairs Cup.'

Football today has become a big business. Keith reflected on the differences between playing in the late 1960s and today.

'It must be quite difficult to motivate yourself now because you are having to play on pride and professionalism to stay up there. The money is there anyway, so they have got that whether they play well or not. So players have got to push themselves to put the performances in and to maintain their profiles. Nowadays, it must be quite a pressurised and different position to be in, I would have thought.'

Keith moved from Newcastle United to Blackpool in 1971 in a deal that saw Tony Green move to St James' Park. Both players sadly had their careers prematurely ended by injury.

'It was sad, really. I was trying to make this comeback and I was finished by the age of 25. I'd got this knee injury and it was quite annoying because I was trying to prove a point by moving away from Newcastle. As a 21-year-old, I'd got the Fairs Cup medal and 100 and odd games under my belt. I could have stayed, but you just think I'll do it somewhere else. I was under pressure when Malcolm Macdonald came to Newcastle. I knew that there was always going to be pressure with him being there, so I thought that I would go and make it somewhere else.

'I was determined to do that, to make it somewhere else. Not getting the chance through injury was quite annoying because Blackpool were nearly back in the First Division then. I would have loved to have been back in the top division. In those days, if you got 10 years out of the game, you had done well. However, you can't look back, you've just got to get on with it.'

Keith Dyson played professionally for Newcastle United, the team that he had supported as a child, for three years. He was a member of the squad that was successful in winning the Inter Cities Fairs Cup in 1969 and to use his own words, 'It was a real honour'. Keith settled in the region after he stopped playing football and nowadays he no longer has to rely on public transport. I would imagine that today he feels a lot more relaxed and happy when he hears people say 'Oh, there's Keith Dyson'.

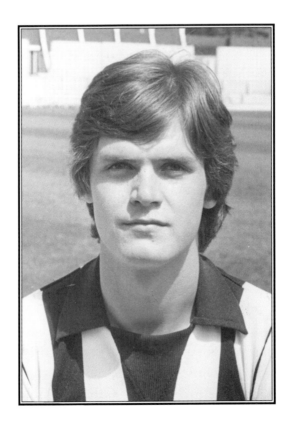

Chapter 10

NIGEL WALKER

(1977–82)

NIGEL Stephen Walker was born in Gateshead on 7 April 1959. He signed professional for Newcastle United in April 1977. A talented midfield player, Nigel made 69 senior starts for Newcastle and scored three goals. Nigel's interest in football began at school.

'It goes right back to junior school, really. I went to

Dunston Junior School, from which another Newcastle United player emerged. That was Ray 'Rocky' Hudson. He was a great lad. He's in America now and has done well for himself. So, I started playing football at junior school.

'When I went to secondary school, it was a rugby playing school, so I actually stopped playing football for a while. At some point, when I must have been 13 or 14, I ended up training with Newcastle. At that time, I had just started playing for Whickham Juniors. I stayed on at school instead of becoming an apprentice and then I eventually signed professional at 18. It was not your conventional sort of route through the system, but that was how it happened for me. To a certain extent, you were usually signed on as a schoolboy.

'When I first started, we used to train up on Hunters Moor. I used to go there two nights a week. The big thing then was that you got changed in the proper dressing room at St James' Park, which was just brilliant, especially for a young kid. Then we used to run up to the Moor to train. I remember on one night in particular, I was introduced to Joe Harvey, which again was a big thrill at the time. I must have been 13 or 14 or something like that. That was a big thing at that age, to be introduced to Joe Harvey. I had been to watch Newcastle play in all the Inter Cities Fairs Cup games, so that was something special, meeting Joe.

'In those days, you were expected to work your way up through the ranks, so to speak. It was very competitive. As you can imagine, lots of kids wanted to do that. I wanted to sign as an apprentice when I was 16, but I was advised to stay on at school, so I did. As I said, I eventually signed professional when I was 18.'

The transition from schoolboy to professional footballer proved to be quite dramatic for Nigel.

'When I signed professional, that was a big change for me, from being a schoolboy to being a pro. On Mondays, they were always very heavy days. You would have had the game on the Saturday, then you would get Sunday off. They would bring you in on the Monday. Basically, they would run you into the ground on that day. Then on the Tuesday it would be a lighter day. Then you would have more football stuff later in the week. So yes, it was a big change for me after I'd signed professional.

'The fitness side of things, they probably do make more of that nowadays, but even in those days, footballers were athletes. Training was fairly rigorous, so it was a big change. In the summer, we used to go to the Bowl in Gateshead. That was something else. Basically, they just ran you for two weeks up the hills and occasionally, you would go down to the beach to do a bit of work on the sand.

'We were at Gateshead one day, a very hot day, because it was usually July when we were back for training. When we got back to the bus to take us back to Benwell, where the training ground used to be, I think that it must have been a combination of the training, the heat, and pure exhaustion, Kevin Carr more or less passed out. We were very worried about him at the time. As it happened, he was alright, but it was a worrying experience, especially for him anyway.

'Pre-season training is hard. It always has been. It always will be, I would imagine. I know that these days they have nutritionists and fitness coaches. They didn't have that level of staff in those days.'

Nigel's recollections of matchdays at St James' Park suggested that the build-up was less frenzied than it is nowadays.

'We used to have to be at the ground for about half past one or two o'clock if it was a home game, with a three o'clock kick-off. You would be at home in the morning. I can't remember doing anything in particular. You would drive across to the ground, park your car, sign a few autographs, walk into the ground, and that was about it. We didn't use to get together for a pre-match meal in those days before a home game. It was never part of the routine.

'Obviously, for away games, it was quite different. If you were at somewhere like Leeds, you would travel on the morning of the game. If not, you would travel away the night before the game. Then you would have a meal together, a light lunch on the Saturday, then you would go on to the game.'

When Nigel signed professional for Newcastle United, he fulfilled the dream of many young lads of playing for the team that he idolised.

'Well, I was a supporter, that's how I started. That is the way that it works for some players, but not many players end up playing for the team that they have supported. I think that the first game I saw at St James' Park was Newcastle United against Manchester United, and George Best was playing. He was my idol as a kid. We used to stand in the Paddock. In those days, obviously, you could just turn up and pay your money. If it was a big game, you had to get across to the ground early and queue. If it wasn't a big game, you could turn up at half past two and you were straight in. In those days, you could more or less get right round the ground, from the Gallowgate End, round the back of the Popular side, right up to the Leazes End. Obviously, that's a massive difference to these days.

'So many of these things happen to you at the wrong time of your life, they happen to you when you're young. You don't really appreciate it as it happens. The first season

I played, in particular when I made my debut, I was just 18. Newcastle were still in the old First Division then. The crowds were massive and it was a massive occasion. It was brilliant, absolutely brilliant, to run out in front of the black and whites. But, unfortunately in terms of timing, I think that I was a little bit unlucky. In that season, we got relegated to the old Second Division. We weren't particularly successful. We had a couple of seasons when we maybe got close to getting promotion, but we never really threatened. Although the crowds always remained big, it was a lower period in Newcastle United's history.'

Nigel made his first-team debut for Newcastle United playing against Bristol City at St James' Park on 5 November 1977. The experience was a bit of a blur.

'It was against Bristol City. It was 1–1. It all goes by so very quickly. I probably couldn't even tell you the team. I could tell you some of the players. The era that I'm talking about was just after Malcolm Macdonald. He had left the previous season, so it was the Gordon Lee, going into the Richard Dinnis era of management. So, there was Alan Gowling, Geoff Nulty, Micky Burns, and Alan Kennedy.'

I asked Nigel if he could recall a particular game that was his favourite.

'There isn't a specific game that stands out. When you look at some of the teams that we played against in that first season, because we were still in the old First Division, we played at the likes of Highbury. We played against Nottingham Forest, Derby County, when they were at the top. I played against some big names.

'I played in a couple of Newcastle-Sunderland derby games and they were always massive games, because they did have that something special, that something extra for me,

especially being a local lad. We always tried to put one over on them. Everyone was so much up for it when we played those games. I remember one derby game at Roker Park, when I think we drew 1–1, and I laid the goal on for Peter Withe. There was also one game when it was 1–1 and we had a chance right towards the death to win it 2–1. There was a clearance off the goal-line, which I had created. That was a good game. That sticks in my memory.'

During his playing career with Newcastle United, Nigel actually scored three goals.

'There was one against Leicester, one against Charlton away. That was funny because as a kid I did use to score a lot of goals, but that never happened at Newcastle. I don't know particularly why, but I'm sure that it might have helped if I'd scored a few more.'

When Nigel moved on from Newcastle in 1982, he joined San Diego in America. I was curious about how the move had come about.

'It was through a reporter actually, Tony Hardesty. He was always a very good friend to me. Things hadn't worked out as well at Newcastle as I would have liked. Arthur Cox, the manager at that time, decided that he wasn't going to offer me another contract. I had heard about one or two things that were happening in this country. Tony Hardesty said "Look, I've got this contact in America, if you're interested in that". It just seemed like a good idea at the time. As it happened, I only stayed out there for just over a year, but I thoroughly enjoyed it. I made a few friends that I've still got now from when I went there. So, in many ways it was a good experience.'

I suggested to Nigel that St James' Park and the game of football had changed dramatically since he played.

'That's an understatement. In one of the more recent games, I was sitting right at the top of the new stand. It was like watching a Subbuteo game. You do get nice views of Gateshead. I think that everyone of whatever age you are at has been nostalgic for an earlier age. One thing that's not so good now is that, if you're a parent, it's not that easy to just decide to take your children to the game on a Saturday. That's just not an option for some people. Whereas, I think most working people would have been able to afford to take their children to the game when I played, but I'm not so sure that's the case these days.

'The money that gets paid out these days, to me that's neither here nor there. Good luck to them. There is a lot of money in the game. Players are a big part of that, so they should be getting a big chunk of it. The behaviour of some of the players when I played wasn't what you would have hoped for. So, I don't think that has changed much over the years. Nowadays it is such a high profile. The only press you came across in those days were the football lads. Football was the only story. Nowadays that is not the case, they are after something else.

'I don't think that loyalty to clubs exists anymore. I think that money has overtaken that. In those days, you would have players who would stay with the same club for 10 years, get their testimonials, and that was right around the country. I think those days have gone, except perhaps for lower down the divisions where you might still have some loyalty.

'Going back to my time, there wasn't a great record of local lads coming through the ranks and making it into the first team. You always felt that if there was someone new who had been bought, they would be played before the local lads. Ray Hudson was a prime example of that. I thought that he was a great player, out of the top drawer. He never really got a look-in at Newcastle. He was always just sort of on the fringe. He went to America and he's done very well out there.'

I asked Nigel about notable opponents from his playing days with Newcastle United.

'The best player that I ever played against in terms of marking was Liam Brady, of Arsenal. He was just out of this world. If you went tight on him, he just played one-touch stuff, and if you'd given him room, he could just pick anything out. He was just an absolutely all-round brilliant player. I played against Archie Gemmell at the City Ground. He was another great player. I played with one or two great players. I thought that Peter Withe was a great player. He went on to play for England. He was a great character as well. You didn't need to go Christmas shopping when you were in the same team as Peter, because his locker used to be full of you name it, he could get you it.'

Nigel had quite a few football heroes.

'George Best, Jimmy Smith, Tony Green, then later, Malcolm Macdonald. 'Jinky' Jimmy Smith, what a player he was. He was a big crowd favourite, but quite rightly so. I remember one game, I think that it was a Boxing Day match against Carlisle. I went to see Newcastle play and 'Jinky' played this ball out of defence to Stewart Barrowclough on the wing. It must have been a 40 to 50-yard ball and he played it with the outside of his foot. It just landed right in Stewart's path. They used to eulogise about Glenn Hoddle, but Jimmy Smith had some of those skills. Maybe he didn't have the full range that Hoddle had, but he was something else.

'Today, you can't go past Alan Shearer. His record speaks for itself, he is just phenomenal. He is still doing it. It shows what a professional he is, when he made that decision not to play for England. You just cannot argue with that.'

During Nigel's time at St James' Park, he experienced mixed fortunes.

'I don't think that I ever got settled to actually have any specific role in the team. I played in a lot of positions, right of midfield, left of midfield, occasionally in the middle of midfield. I suppose I was more of a creative midfield player rather than a defensive midfield player.

'I enjoyed it all at the time. I enjoy looking back on it. Things could have gone better for me, things could have gone a hell of a lot worse. I did it, I ran out there at St James' Park. It's an experience that you cannot take away. It did mean a lot to me.

'I think that the worst moment was a cup match at Exeter. I was substitute in the game at home, I think, when we drew 1–1. I came on and laid a goal on for Alan Shoulder. We went down to Exeter and it was 4–0. It was a nightmare. It was one of those games when everyone was below par. As always, we had good travelling support, so that was a bad night. Obviously, being relegated in my first season was a low point.

'When I've looked back and thought about why I didn't perhaps do as well as some people thought I might have done, I think that I was unlucky as well in the managers who were there at the time. As with a lot of things, a little bit of luck comes into play. After I left Newcastle and went to America, I remember my brother rang me up and literally said "They have just signed Kevin Keegan". I had just headed off across the Atlantic. My timing was just a little bit off there.

'I was there when Chris Waddle was signed, so I remember the first season that he came in. It was just so obvious straightaway that here was a lad who could play. He was very similar in some respects to John Connolly. John had this knack of going at a full-back and he wouldn't touch the ball, but he would do something with his body and the full-back would more or less fall over. 'Waddler' used to be able to do the same thing. It was very effective. Newcastle supporters have always liked exciting football and exciting players. They would much rather watch a 4–3 victory than 1–0.'

'I don't miss it at all, really. I've got a very nice life now. I really enjoy myself. I'm a teacher, which I enjoy. I've got a lovely wife and a lovely family, and things have worked out well in that respect. I was a footballer for 10 years. I made a living out of it for 10 years and I made some very good friends out of it. I've also got a lot of good memories from it.

'I was at Newcastle for five years, in America for one year, then in various parts of the country after that, which was interesting. Obviously, the career path didn't go the way I planned it, but I wouldn't have changed it. When I stopped playing professional, I played non-league for 10 years after that, so it wasn't as though I'd given it up. I was a professional until I was 28, then I played non-league until I was 38, so I kept training. I had five years at Blyth, which was brilliant. There were some great lads up there. I had a couple of years down at Dunston Fed, which was again great. So, I've seen all sorts of levels of local football.'

When Nigel looks back over his football career, he is able to reflect upon the highs and the lows. He admits to having enjoyed much of his playing days. He also values all that has happened since he stopped playing football. Nigel was fortunate to have been given the opportunity to play for the club that he had supported as a youngster, fulfilling the dream. If he had been born only a couple of years later, he might have found himself playing with a very different squad. As Nigel himself said, 'My timing was just a little bit off'.

Chapter 11

DAVID McCREERY
(1982–89)

DAVID McCreery was born in Belfast, Northern Ireland on 16 September 1957. He graduated through the youth academy at Old Trafford and was an FA Cup finalist in 1976 and an FA Cup winner in 1977 with Manchester United. He played for his country in the World Cup Finals in 1982 and 1986 and during his football career, he gained 67 full international caps. David signed for Newcastle United from the Tulsa Roughnecks in the US in October 1982 for £75,000. He made 266 senior starts for Newcastle United and scored two goals. The foundations of David's football career began when he was a teenager living in Northern Ireland.

'I started off obviously in Belfast and it was a case of I went for trial at Manchester United. First of all, I went for two weeks and then the following summer I got invited over for six weeks. Then I signed associate schoolboy forms. Then I started going over the summer holidays and it got to the stage when I was 14 or 15, Manchester United youth team used to send over for me, and I used to fly over from school. I used to get two days a week off school and go and play football with the youth team, which was a big thing for a boy of only 14 or 15. I kept going over and they offered me an apprenticeship which I did after I left school.'

Following the recent completion of the new purpose-built Newcastle United training facilities, I asked David for his memories of the training facilities and regime at the time he was playing.

'To be truthful, training was very good. I always enjoyed training, but facility wise, by today's standards it was horrendous. At Benwell there were just two changing rooms and you had a peg. It was like being at school. There was an old gentleman there called Ronnie who made the tea before and after training. It was like in a little kitchen. The gymnasium was just like a building with Astroturf inside, and that was the gym. I think it was really basic compared to what it is now. If players can't play now, there's something wrong.

'After a game, we would be in on the Monday. It would be quite hard. Once the season started, it wasn't so bad, but at the start of the season, you'd be in twice a day. Then it would be tapered down to once a day. Then you'd be in at about a quarter to nine, or maybe 10 o'clock, have a laugh with the lads, have a cup of tea or whatever. You'd go out and train and finish maybe at half 12, one o'clock. Then in the afternoon, that was it. You did what everyone else did. You were free for the rest of the day.

'I would say that on the Monday it would be the hardest one, coming back in after a game, depending on whether it had been a good result or a bad result on the Saturday. It was more about fitness. Then on the Tuesday, it was football. Sometimes, if it was a good week, you'd maybe have the Wednesday off, and be back in on the Thursday. Then it was set pieces or whatever on the Thursday, concentrating on the game coming up on the Saturday.'

Over the years, the build-up to games changed, as did the individual routines of the players. Given the robust nature of David's style of play, he was often receiving treatment right up to the last moment.

'For me, if it was a home game, I always stuck to the same routine. It was maybe a case of get up at half nine or 10 o'clock and have a bit of breakfast. We probably had to report in at about half 12. Home games, sometimes if there were big games, we'd have a pre-match meal at the Swallow Hotel.

'I used to like to get there early, to get everything sorted out, make sure all my kit was there. Sometimes, if I'd had knocks, I've seen myself on the treatment table in the morning to have treatment, to see whether I was going to play on the Saturday afternoon. I'd go and see the physio, get the okay from him, go and have a cup of tea, then go to the game.'

Most footballers will admit to having some little superstitions and it was widely believed that David wore special socks when playing for Newcastle United. The reality was a little different.

'Most of the time I used to wear completely black socks. It was purely because we had the white-topped ones and they were very tight on my legs. I had short legs and the black socks were more comfortable. It was nothing more than that.'

David arrived in Newcastle after playing in America. I asked him to recall his early memories of the stadium and the supporters.

'I think that it's a case of it was unbelievable. We used to walk straight into the reception. Nowadays, you have to go through so much security. I always remember the wire fence. We had the wire fencing round the pitch. In those days, they were frightened of people running on to the field. Nowadays, with all the season tickets, people wouldn't dare run on to the field for fear of being banned. In this area, you know how much they enjoy their football. But it was always the fencing that springs to mind.

'I always remember when we clinched promotion at Huddersfield in 1984. I'll never forget it because we played in the grey and silver kit. We came off the field shoulder high. It was an incredible feeling. It was the same when we beat Manchester City 5–0. I think when we went out that night, we couldn't go into anywhere without people lifting you shoulder high.

'The supporters at that time, they were the best in the country. They were the most loyal and the most knowledge-able. They were also the most local. Do you remember the 'Sack the Board' era? Sometimes you'd get that, but 95 percent of the time the crowd were with you. Some of the travelling support in the First Division made it feel like a home game. The hair on the back of your neck would stand on end. Even now, it happens when you're sitting in the stands.'

David was a midfield general on the field and he had a reputation for never shirking a challenge. He was quite modest about his role in the team.

'When I went to Newcastle after I'd been in America, I could've signed for Real Sociedad just after the 1982 World Cup. But Arthur Cox and Stan Seymour came on the phone and they were saying "We've got Kevin Keegan and Terry McDermott". It was a case of adapting to those sorts of players.

'Playing for Northern Ireland in the 1982 World Cup, it was my job to win the ball and give it to other people. I had a rest after that. Playing for Newcastle, it was a case of I won the ball and gave it to the likes of Chris Waddle, Kevin Keegan, Terry McDermott and Peter Beardsley. Then I had my rest. It was my job, if an attack broke down, to win the ball back again and get it up front again, if you know what I mean. I enjoyed that. I enjoyed it that way. It was winning the ball and giving it to the players who could play.'

Although he saw his role as essentially a ball-winner for other players, David did agree that he could 'play a bit' himself. During the promotion season of 1983/84, David was at the heart of a midfield that defended, dominated, and created for an exciting forward line. David was noted for his fearless approach to the game and he would regularly throw himself into tackles that left opponents somewhat bewildered.

David actually scored two goals for Newcastle United and it seemed unfair to ask him to choose which was his favourite, so I asked him to relive them both.

'The first one, I think my wife had a heart attack. It was from about one yard out. I think that Steve Carney and I scored at Leicester. Then I scored at Tottenham. It was a half volley from just outside the box. I used to get a nosebleed when I used to get up that far up the field. When I got there, Kevin and Terry

133

Mac would be saying "Get back". I should have scored more goals really, but it was more my job to defend.'

David was in no doubt that his career highlight was playing for his country, Northern Ireland, in the World Cup Finals in 1982.

'I would say the 1982 World Cup was the highlight, when we went on to qualify for the quarter-finals. Going away with Northern Ireland, a lot of people said we were travelling with just a toothbrush. In fact, I don't think the Northern Ireland FA booked any hotel rooms for if we qualified. I think that once we had qualified, they were searching around to try to get rooms. But, I would say that the '82 World Cup was the highlight because we were up against it, you know, all the time, and once with 10 men as well.'

When David signed for Newcastle United, Arthur Cox was the manager and he held him in high regard.

'Arthur was a disciplinarian, but he was fair with it. If you gave your lot, he gave the same back to you. I'll never forget the time when I had a very bad injury, when I had 60 stitches in my leg. And after that, there was another game against Leeds when Arthur must have thought that I was very brave or probably more stupid.

'I went up to head a ball with Frank Worthington and he caught me with the elbow and cut my eye. It was streaming with blood and the physio came running up the touchline, saying "I'll have to take him off, you know". So, as I was getting treatment, expecting to go off, Arthur Cox came running up and looked at me. He just stuck his hand in a jar of Vaseline, smeared it on, and pushed me back on again. It was things like that, but he knew how to treat players. Again, he knew the ones to put an arm round and the ones who needed a kick up the backside.'

I asked David to look back over his playing career and to reveal his heroes and villains. There was one clear hero.

'George Best. I had the opportunity to play four internationals with him. For me, he was the best. At the same time, he was the reason for me going to Manchester United. I had the same opportunity to go to Tottenham as a schoolboy, to sign schoolboy forms. I think it was because he was from Belfast, it was the reason why.

'As I said, I had the opportunity to play four internationals with him. He was a lovely guy. He was just a diamond. When he came in with us in the Irish squad, there were no airs or graces. He just mucked in. The manager was Danny Blanchflower, so it was interesting meeting for the team talks. He would say "Just give the ball to George,"and that was it.

'Opponents, I think that it was probably Graeme Souness and Jimmy Case, when we played against Liverpool. I don't think I ever got the better of them. They won a lot of trophies, but then again we were playing a Liverpool team who were superb.'

During all players' careers, there are inevitably memories of highs and lows, and some moments that are often forgotten, or even best forgotten. Like most players, David was able to remember some moments that were either amusing or embarrassing.

'I scored an own-goal once against Chelsea when Glenn Roeder tried to clear the ball off the line and it hit me on the knee. Now that was embarrassing.

'Do you remember the famous photo of Vinny Jones grabbing Gazza [Paul Gascoigne] by the goolies? Paul was so frightened. He was telling the boys afterwards that Vinny went beside him, saying "I'm after you tonight", then he'd go away and take a throw-in. Paul would be looking, concentrating, and he'd come back and say "I'm back". He was really on him that night. Paul was scared all through that game.

'I remember again with Paul, I think he had Kevin Keegan's boots. He took Kevin Keegan's boots home to clean and he lost them on the bus, or at least he lost one of them on the bus.

'I remember with John Bailey, we went over to Trinidad and Tobago to play at the end of the season and John was playing left-back. We played at the Trinidad and Tobago cricket ground, which was so open, and it must have been 100 and odd degrees. John was left-back and he would never tuck in. He used to stand in the shade. We actually lost two goals with them coming in the inside of the left-back. John would always stand in the shade because it was so hot.

'When we went to Bermuda, we played the national team, I think, it was the summer break. Everybody had been out the night before, but it was a practice game as such. John Bailey was playing and he started to be sick. Everybody was going to get a game, so John came over to Willie McFaul who took him off, he was so bad. He sat down and turned round to Willie and said "Gaffer, it must have been that fish I had last night". He'd had a few drinks, you know what I mean.'

In the world of football, things are somewhat different nowadays compared to when David played in the 1980s.

'Players then were players, you know. You got your money's worth out of them. You got your blood, sweat and tears. Nowadays you're a star, if you know what I mean. You have young players on big contracts and they have nothing to achieve. Because they are on so much money now, there is no incentive to jump from the reserves.

'When I was an apprentice at Manchester United, you had to clean the boots, the changing rooms, the toilets, and do the training gear. I remember cleaning Martin Buchan's boots. If they weren't clean enough, you'd get them back to clean again. Nowadays they have kit men. They should go back to the old apprenticeships.'

After commencing his football career with Manchester United, David was transferred to Queens Park Rangers in 1979. He subsequently moved to America in 1981 where he played for the Tulsa Roughnecks. Playing in Oklahoma was somewhat different to playing at Loftus Road in London W12. David's next football move back to England proved to be an equally contrasting experience.

'I was playing for the Tulsa Roughnecks and I still had my house in London, rented out or whatever. We came back and I was supposed to meet Joe Harvey. He phoned up and I remember that my mother-in-law was living with us at the time. I think she may have answered the phone. I tried to get to see Joe, but I missed my flight twice. I got a third flight and eventually met with Joe. We went to Joe's house and I signed for Newcastle, then I flew back home again.

'I remember my wife and I coming to Newcastle, after living in America in 90 degrees heat, and coming over the Tyne Bridge we were thinking 'Oh my God'. It was a real change, but I've been here for 20 years and I've really enjoyed it. I wouldn't leave now. When you first arrive after you've been flying over, you're bound to be really apprehensive.

'When I first came to Newcastle, you couldn't see the ground, and I had to find it. I moved into a house in the Morpeth area when I first signed. When I had my first home game at St James' Park, I didn't know how to get to the ground from where I was living in Morpeth. It was a night game, so it was dark. I'll never forget it, I stopped at the Cowgate roundabout because I didn't know where to go next.

'I stopped two lads at the bus stop and said "Excuse me, can you tell me where the ground is?" I saw that they were wearing scarves. Of course, they were going to the game, so they took me there. I gave them a lift, would you believe. I think in the end they realised who I was. But would you believe it, a gentleman came to do the electrical work where I work years later and he said "Do you remember me?" He was one of the lads that I gave a lift to.

'I remembered stopping to ask for directions to the ground and thinking that they must've thought it was a bit stupid. You know, if I couldn't find my way to the ground, how on earth was I going to find my way round the pitch. I didn't stop anybody after that. I managed to avoid getting lost again.'

David played for Newcastle United for almost seven years and was a favourite with the supporters, being respected for his no-nonsense determination to succeed. He would boldly go where many players would never dream of going. It was sometimes a painful experience, but this was something that David accepted as part of the game. He was content to throw himself into the tackle, and if necessary get patched up and get on with it.

Although David joked that he was still waiting for another growth spurt, to most supporters he was a giant of a player. Looking back over his years at St James' Park, David probably covered every inch of the pitch. Fortunately, he only got lost on one occasion, and that was before he put on his 'lucky' black socks.

Chapter 12

JOHN BERESFORD
(1992–98)

JOHN Beresford was born in Sheffield on 4 September 1966. He signed for Newcastle United from Portsmouth in June 1992 for £650,000. John played at left-back, making 227 senior starts and scoring eight goals. Taking John back to his childhood, it was clear that football was in his blood. This is how it all began.

'Literally as a kid, your best mate was the lad who'd got a football. I mean, it's changed a little these days, but you'd go into a park or on a street and just play football. I was lucky enough that my father was a footballer, though he was finished through injury at 21 really as a professional, and he gave me an unbelievable amount of encouragement. In a sense, he made me what I am today.

'We were totally different players, but I suppose he sort of gave me the drive to achieve more than he ever did. As a kid, that was it. You know, the icon at the time was Kevin Keegan for me. I had the poster on the wall and my mother fancied him, that kind of thing. It was kind of weird, moving on to like 25 years later, you think to yourself, hang on a bit, I'm actually playing for this person who was my idol.

'But that was it. That's how I got into football. I'd played for the city, as in Sheffield Boys, then I was lucky enough to be selected for Yorkshire Boys, then England Schoolboys. Then you think to yourself that it's all panned out and you're going to be a professional footballer.'

Sadly for John, his dream was to be turned into a nightmare, just when he thought that everything was mapped out for him.

'But then what happened was I went to Manchester City as a kid. Malcolm Allison had set up a youth policy. He was like the forerunner of how to get the cream of the crop, especially from around the northern area. But Billy McNeill was the manager then and he actually made a mess of it, he cocked it all up.

'I think he must've released at least five players for about £150,000 who all went on to play for England and all made a lot of money. He didn't give the kids a chance at the time. Alex Ferguson realised this when he took over at

Manchester United. He turned it on its head and when you look at how they are now, they've reaped the rewards.

'So I had a big fallout with Billy McNeill at the time. I was in England Schoolboys, so I was supposedly one of the better players for my age at that time in the country. Then within six months, I was told that I wasn't good enough and was thrown on the scrapheap. So then, you have to sort of rebuild your career as such, because it's a bit of a knock to the system. You have to try to build your confidence up.'

Fortunately for John, he was soon given another chance to pursue his love for football and his desire to succeed.

'I was lucky enough, I went to Barnsley. Alan Clarke took me there. Talk about a shock to the system, that really was. I mean, I'd literally been at a big club and all of a sudden, you were penny-pinching. But, for me it was great. I was back to doing what I loved, I was playing football.

'I had three great years there. Glory football it wasn't, but then we weren't a great team. They took you down the pit to show you how lucky you were. I have to hold my hands up, what a working environment that was. I could not believe what I saw down there. In a sense, it gave you that little push. For me, I thought it was a great idea just to show us how lucky we were. You shouldn't take it all for granted.'

After his three years with Barnsley, John found himself on the move to the south coast.

'Sold from Barnsley to Portsmouth for £300,000. I bought their new floodlights. That was the reason that I was sold, just to make some money. John Gregory signed me at Portsmouth, but he tried to make too many changes too quickly. We had four managers at Portsmouth in a short space of time. It wasn't until Jim Smith took over that the club was sorted out.

'I was just starting to get noticed at that point. We were lucky enough to have an FA Cup run which put us in the spotlight. We lost in the semi-final on penalties to Liverpool after a replay, so we had a lot of coverage. Then all of a sudden I was about to sign for Liverpool.'

John found himself on the verge of heading for the big time by signing for a big club, only to have the dream shattered then rescued in somewhat dramatic style.

'There I was, driving to Anfield with my dad, contract sorted out, all the press waiting, just needing to have a medical. I was thinking to myself that this was it, my dream come true. Then, all of a sudden I was told that I had failed the medical.

'As you can guess, I was on my knees, I was so disappointed. I'd had this dream of playing in red and playing in front of the Kop. I was going to have to go back to Portsmouth. I later found out that the failed medical had nothing to do with my fitness. There had been a problem between the board and manager and I got caught up in it.

'Then I got this phone call and it's Kevin Keegan. I'm thinking that it's a windup. Anyway, he asked to see me, so I drive down to London because he was at Ascot at the races. When we met, he had a top hat and tails on and everything. I'll always remember the conversation. He said "I'm going to get this club, Newcastle United, into the Premiership and into Europe, and I'm going to make you into an England international."

'I remember thinking, are you sure? Newcastle had nearly gone down to the Third Division. I'd played against them for Portsmouth and no disrespect, but they weren't very good. Keegan had inherited this team and he saved them.

He needed to buy a lot of new players for what he was talking about. I give him his due, when he talks he really believes in what he's trying to do. And he lets you know it.

'By the time we played the first game against Bruges in Europe and I'd got into the England squad, he said to me "You thought that I was joking, didn't you? I'm going to make this club one of the biggest in the world." To be honest, he made it what it is today. Don't get me wrong, Sir John Hall gave him the opportunity, but Keegan's the reason why Newcastle is what it is.'

I recalled taking my own sons down to watch Newcastle United players train at Maiden Castle, Durham, and John had fond memories of what was at the time a unique experience.

'I know that training regimes have changed over the years. Nowadays you concentrate on nutrition a little bit more and a bit more stretching, thinking how you can get more performance-wise. I always worked on it, it was the style of game I had. I needed to work on my fitness.

'But what made it so enjoyable, if you turned up for training and you saw hundreds and thousands of people coming up to watch you, you didn't need a lift. Whether it's pouring down with rain or freezing cold and you see these people have come out, it doesn't half give you a buzz. I can't thank the people enough for when they came down to watch us.

'You see the kids and they want an autograph. Yes it can be frustrating when you're stood for an hour after training and you just want to get home and it's freezing cold. But Keegan created that because he knew that certain people couldn't get tickets for the games. So he said "Well, if you can't watch the games, come round to training, you're more than welcome." To make it an open house like that, I thought that was just a special thing.

'People would say that some players don't like that too close proximity, but I thought it was a great thing. It gave me a chance to meet the supporters. I think footballers sometimes get a little detached from the supporters, especially now that they're overprotected. You don't get a chance to actually talk to the supporters, you don't get to understand what it means to them.

'I knew that Newcastle was a big club, but you don't realise it until you actually live there, and you breathe it by mixing with the locals. I remember from the training for the first build-up to the Sunderland derby, you realise just what it means. Men, women, children, pensioners, were all saying "Don't let us down, not on this one." That made you understand that you must associate with your supporters. I think it was a great help for Keegan to do that with the training. It helped us tremendously.'

There are many stories of players having superstitions on matchdays and John was no exception.

'I always say that players lie if they say they haven't got little superstitions. Everyone's got their own little quirks. Myself, I would eat the same things. The night before a game, I would usually have fish and a bit of pasta. In the morning, it was beans on toast. You don't like to change it.

'When I pulled up in my car outside the ground or wherever we were parking, because it changed over the years, I could not get out unless the song playing had finished. The song had to finish, whether it had just started or was nearly over, when I pulled up. I can remember people looking and on odd occasions, you'd get reporters outside wondering if you were ever going to get out of the car.

'Then in the changing room, you'd get changed in certain ways. My right boot always went on first, my left shinpad always went on first, and my right tie-up was always a little longer than the other one. They were my little quirks. Everybody's got something, I do believe that. When you really ask them, some of them will say "No, no, no, well I do this and I do that." It's a mental thing, it really is. I think football now is changing. They bring in psychologists and all it is, is you feel as though you're mentally prepared, that's the difference nowadays, football could be a little bit more focused.

'The other side of it, in years gone by, say 20 years before I played, players were a lot mentally stronger, because I think that they had a harder upbringing. So, it's a catch 22 trying to get the right level. I think in a footballing sense we were like tarts really compared to the old-style players. They used to get kicked, get stitched up, get back on the pitch, and get kicked again. I think again that it's a mental thing. You're pampered a little bit more nowadays. So, it's swings and roundabouts trying to get the right balance.'

In 1992, John went from the major shock of not signing for Liverpool to the rollercoaster ride of becoming a key player in Kevin Keegan's squad, aptly nicknamed the 'Entertainers', who won the First Division title and earned their place back in the big time.

'I've never seen anything like it. Ten wins on the trot and you're thinking to yourself, it doesn't get any better than this. But, it wasn't just that, it was the training, the way Kevin was, the way he created such a buzz. He created such a belief, not just in the players but in the supporters and everyone around him.

'There wasn't one day that I can ever think of, when you didn't want to come in because of the atmosphere and the spirit in the place. The lads were always laughing and joking. Yes, you worked very hard, but it was just so enjoyable. Keegan didn't have a problem with laughing and joking in training. You get some managers who would think that you're not working hard enough, so they would run you more. Keegan used to be very clever. He would say to players, if he felt that they hadn't put the effort in during training, "I hope you're saving it for Saturday." He wouldn't be ranting or raving, he would just have a quiet word. All of a sudden, the pace would be picked up.

'In training, Keegan believed in playing at match tempo. Every new signing who arrived over that period took probably a month to six weeks to get used to the pace of training. At other clubs, you would find that training was a little bit slower or dragged out a lot, but at Newcastle it was high tempo, with a lot of small-sided games. When you came to the game on Saturdays, it seemed to be easier, because you felt as though you'd got a bit more time and space. It did make a difference.'

During the 1995/96 season, Newcastle United seemed destined to win the championship for the first time since 1927. Sadly, as history shows, a significant lead was eroded by Manchester United, who clinched the title by four points.

'It was a mighty blow, but we gave it everything. I think that the team had learned from it and Kevin had learned from it. Then the following season, when the cracks started to appear a little bit, I was just so disappointed that Kevin moved out when he did. It takes you a while. Because we did so well so early, we had created a monster.

'From a player's point of view and from the club's point of view, we were just there too early. If we had just stuck in there, maybe we wouldn't have won it the following season, but we could have gained the confidence to get closer to Manchester United. Looking back over history, Alex Ferguson was so close to getting the sack. It takes you a while.'

Newcastle United met Manchester United in the Charity Shield, the traditional curtain-raiser to the football season, in August 1996 and were well-beaten 4–0. It was no surprise that revenge was in the air when the two teams met at St James' Park on 20 October 1996, playing in front of a capacity crowd of 36,579 and a worldwide television audience. It was a day to remember. To Newcastle United supporters it will always be known as the '5–0'.

'There was a lot of tension before the game because we felt we owed the fans because of the Charity Shield. We'd let them and the club down. In football, if you're playing well, you usually have six or seven players on top of their game, one or two okay, and you'll get the odd player who's not. It's the law of averages. On that night, everyone was up for it. Everything kicked into place, the team sort of gelled and we showed just what we were all about.

'I really did believe after that game that we had learned from the experiences of the previous season, had a better squad, and we were right to win the title, if we could stay away from injuries. It just came together that night. I remember, as soon as we got the first goal, that meant that Manchester United had to come out and that was what Newcastle was all about. It made the game open and when we were at our best, we could destroy anybody.

'You've got to realise, we used to take some stick at the back because we played a certain way. People used to say "They can't defend". It wasn't the fact that we couldn't defend, we were told not to defend, as in a so-called Arsenal way. We weren't told to sit back. Keegan believed that we were going to score more goals than them. Yes, you defended in certain ways, but the style we played, you're always going to be liable to the sucker punch when you leave space at the back.

'I remember speaking to Ryan Giggs in the players' lounge after the game and he said "I'm stunned. I just cannot believe what's just happened. We've actually played quite well. You've just absolutely battered us". Manchester United actually had a couple of chances. The score should really have been about 9–2. That's how easily it could have gone.'

Unfortunately, Newcastle's season soon took a turn for the worse.

'It was a nightmare. Alan Shearer got injured straight after the game and Les Ferdinand got injured during the following game. You can say it's ifs and buts, but that's when you learn that you need a big squad if you want to get to the top and stay there. Certain players you can carry, others you can't. If you look back, we didn't have a big squad and that was the problem with it. But to finish second twice on the run to Manchester United showed how close we were getting.'

During the 1997/98 season, John added a new dimension to his game. Already an experienced left-back, he suddenly became a surprise goalscorer, especially in the European games.

'You just find yourself having a purple patch. But also my game changed a little bit. We were playing in a sense at that time with three centre-halves. People knew that I used to bomb on, but it was really to give the ball to people like Andy Cole, David Ginola, Peter Beardsley, Les Ferdinand and Alan Shearer. Then what happened was when Kenny Dalglish took over, I had the licence not just to get the ball to the edge of the penalty area and create for others, but to go forward and get into the box. That was the difference, you could find yourself getting into more advanced areas.

'I was very fit, so I didn't mind breaking my neck to get into the box, sometimes running 70 yards. I worked on the law of averages. I maybe didn't have the ability of a centre-forward, but I thought if I keep getting in there, sooner or later that ball will fall at my feet. As it happened, I did have that sort of run. I was lucky enough to get on the end of things in big games, vital games, especially the Champions League like Croatia Zagreb and away at Kiev. In a sense, I could have had twice as many.

'I remember going to a press conference in the Champions League and I was hearing "The top goalscorers at the moment are Rivaldo, Tino Asprilla, and John Beresford". For me, it was nice to hear that, to be named in that league.'

Newcastle United supporters, the Toon Army, are well-known worldwide for their fanatical support and loyalty. John recalls what he felt during his playing days in the city.

'It's hard to explain. The nearest I can say is it's like a religion. I do believe that. You're brought up on it, through parents and grandparents, or whoever. I come from a footballing city, Sheffield, but the intensity is nowhere near like it is in Newcastle. You have to live it. I used to love going out. Going back to the '5–0', I was straight into the town celebrating. You'd walk straight into the clubs and people were applauding you and were wanting to talk to you. You just got the feel of the place and what it meant to them.

'Our sponsorship used to be Newcastle Brewery and they used to wait for the result before they sent out the alcohol to the pubs, especially when we were playing away from home. It was three times as much if Newcastle had won. So, that shows the effect it had on the people.'

All players will have memories of their playing career, some good, some not so good. John was asked to recall his best performance and best goal.

'I would have to say that my best performance was away at Everton in the league. I actually got injured towards the end. I'd pulled my hamstring. I remember Keegan saying "That is the nearest to the perfect game I've ever seen you play. You never gave the ball away in your interceptions and your tackles." I remember thinking to myself that I didn't do anything wrong. Everything that I did was spot on.

'I would have to say that my best goal was against Aston Villa. There was a corner that finished up with the ball being headed out. I took it on my thigh and volleyed it into the top corner of the net. To my surprise, it went in. It caught the underside of the bar, which always makes it look a little bit more dramatic. It was during the season that I was getting on the end of things. I remember that my first goal was a penalty against Barnsley. It's always special to get your first goal for your new club.

'I'll tell you what was just unbelievable and it's so clear to me, Barcelona at home in the Champions League first game. To me, I just thought this is the big time. I was playing against Luis Figo and all the rest. I remember the build-up to it and the noise was electric. The game itself was just unbelievable, typical Newcastle game, 3–2. In the

dressing room, everybody was buzzing. I went down town afterwards and the place was jumping. The supporters felt that they were part of something special and I was lucky enough to have been a part of it.'

As a defender, John was faced with some difficult opponents and he highlighted a couple of the more formidable.

'I hated playing against Chris Waddle. He played on the right and he was so heavily left-footed. You always knew the trick. He used to drop his shoulder, but he used to go with it so much, you'd finish up going with it as well. He was probably the most difficult skill-wise.

'One player who was hard work, running for 90 minutes, was Andrei Kanchelskis. He was very strong and very quick, and you knew that you were in for a tough time. When he got the ball, he used to run at you at 100 miles an hour and you had to be on your toes for the whole game. Most attackers don't like defending. With my game, playing against certain wingers, I used to run them to tire them out.'

John has often said that signing for Newcastle United was his greatest career moment and he still holds Kevin Keegan in very high regard. However, the two of them had their moments, with perhaps the most famous being captured on national television. It was Newcastle United at home against Aston Villa and the game had barely got going.

'It was just the pressure of the Premiership. We were just starting to slide slightly. It started on the Friday when Kevin said to me "Look, Aston Villa play three up front, so I want you to tuck in more and help the centre-halves out because they play with wing-backs."

'The problem we had was Gary Charles was playing wing-back and I knew that he would bomb on. So I said

"Daveed [David Ginola] isn't going to come back." The one thing we always knew about Daveed was that he was great with the ball, but without it, he was not the best. Kevin said "No, I'll have a word with him, he'll be fine." I said "He won't come back, I know he won't." Kevin said "Look, he will, just do as you're told."

'So, usual thing, game kicks off, I tucked in and Gary Charles bombs on, the cross comes in and goes out for a corner. Kevin starts shouting "You're too far in." I went "I'm not ******* too far in. You said that Daveed was going to ******* look after Gary Charles." He said "Just get on with it."

'It happens again and Kevin shouts again. I turned to the bench and went "I've ******* told you." Well, unknown to me, Kevin had family sitting near the bench. I remember seeing him going to get the numbers out and I knew I'd probably got two minutes or so to score a hat-trick so I could stay on that pitch.

'As I was walking off the pitch, I was thinking, I can't take this back. People over time will know that with Kevin, if you upset him, you've got a long way back. Put it this way, I've never been as fit, never worked so hard over that next pre-season, to actually grovel to be given one more chance.

'He set an example and not many lads actually spoke to him that way again. That's the reason. It was good management. At the time, I thought he was out of order, he didn't give me a second chance. The game was only 15 minutes old, but I understood where he was coming from.

'We even laugh about it now. I played in Matt Le Tissier's testimonial match and Kevin was the manager of our team. He said "Bez, if I ask you to come off, you're not going to swear at me are you?"

John moved to Southampton in 1998 after what he regarded as an unbelievable seven years of football.

'Playing at Newcastle for Kevin Keegan was very special for me. I can't praise him enough. I still hope that one day he'll return to Newcastle and finish the job that he started.'

Postscript

THE FINAL WHISTLE

THE recollections of the 12 players featured in this book have covered a period of some 54 years, from the days of the old shaky grainy black and white cine films to the era of high-tech satellite television. Mirroring this progress in broadcasting, we have also witnessed several developments on and off the football field. Looking back over the years, certain aspects of football have changed quite dramatically.

Football pitches today contribute to faster games and more skilful ball control. Teams of groundsmen are employed to nurture every blade of grass. Replacing a divot is regarded as an art form. The creative designs produced by the lawnmowers are masterpieces to be admired by adoring millions. Once the undersoil heating is switched on, it must be like cuddling up with hundreds of hot water bottles. Life on the football field today is a far more comfortable experience than it was during the days of playing on top of several inches of mud.

Training facilities are now purpose-built and state of the art. Sophisticated gymnasiums ensure that fitness levels are maintained to a high standard. Teams of physiotherapists help to soothe aching limbs and repair torn muscles. Nutrition experts ensure that healthy diets are adhered to. Indoor football pitches allow uninterrupted preparations for those important games when the ground outside is frozen solid or covered with six inches of snow.

Professional footballers nowadays are able to leave the comfort of their more than comfortable houses and drive their new sponsored cars to training or home games. Gone are the days of having to stand in the queue at a bus stop, only to discover when you have completed your journey through numerous mining villages that you didn't even get a place on the substitutes' bench.

Premiership football stadiums are now all-seater monsters, with modern designs seemingly stolen from the discarded ideas of science fiction illustrators. The Hillsborough disaster led to the eventual dismantling of the wire fences and the demise of terraces occupied by standing football supporters. It was appropriate at the time to review the safety standards at football grounds and significant changes inevitably followed the publication of the Taylor Report.

Since watching football today requires you to remain in your seat, the opportunity to leap in the air when your team scores a goal brings some welcome relief to numb buttocks. It also gives you the chance to stretch your legs. Of course, you are now obliged to visit the designated toilets when in need of a different kind of relief, since urinating on the terraces is no longer permitted. The disadvantage of having to leave your seat is that you might miss a goal. However, an obvious advantage is that your shoes might stay dry.

The requirement to replace the open terraces with all-seater stands led to the increased use of the season ticket schemes, which ultimately saw capacities come down and waiting lists go up. The days of turning up at your local ground 30 minutes before kick-off and paying at the turnstiles are long gone. The days of fathers taking their sons to matches when they can afford to do so are also long gone. Now you wait your turn and then pay out hundreds of pounds, often before the previous season has become a memory.

Professional footballers today have the opportunity to lead the life of a superstar. They can acquire the same status as a Hollywood actor. To their managers and agents, footballers are prize assets, to be protected at all times. It can now be difficult for supporters to get autographs of players unless they are face to face with them. Letters to players via their clubs are often unsuccessful because of paranoia that every request is from some dealer trying to make a few more pounds on the Internet. It should perhaps be remembered that without a paying public, football clubs could face financial hardship.

It is sad that the lifestyle led by many professional footballers today has led to a significant distancing of themselves from the supporters. Some players cannot cope with this lifestyle and hit the headlines for all the wrong reasons. Of course, they will soon realise that they have fallen on hard times when their autographs bounce.

Throughout the interviews carried out for this book, I did not encounter any of the distancing to which I referred earlier. I simply located 12 former players, contacted them by telephone, requested an interview for a book, arranged to do it, and then encouraged them to recall their playing days. They could not have been more accommodating or helpful.

For me, this book has highlighted the good and bad things that we have lost from football under the guise of progress. To the players featured in these pages, football was a job and whatever they were paid, they always did their best. They also did not distance themselves from the supporters. Commitment and loyalty seem to be lacking in the modern game, with players no longer needing to wait around for their testimonials.

There has been much written in fanzines and newspapers about the lack of atmosphere in the new all-seater stadiums. The impact of singing has been reduced by the current system of season ticket allocations. Supporters are almost afraid to open their mouths for fear of some zealous steward deciding that they are being abusive. Generating an atmosphere from a sitting position in virtual silence is not very easy.

Football today is a business, a big business. It is a far cry from the days when local lads used to cheer on local lads. Times have changed. I started watching football in an era when, as I recall, we stood on the terraces, packed in together, singing together, and cheering together. It didn't matter if your terrace neighbour was a business executive or a retired docker, we were all there for the same reason, to give our team our undivided attention and our full support.

I hope that this book has brought back special Magpie memories of what, for many, were the 'good old days' at St James' Park.